How to Ignite Your Passion for Living

The Sure-Fire Formula to Getting What You REALLY Want

Mark O. Haroldsen

HOW TO IGNITE YOUR PASSION FOR LIVING
Copyright © 2009 by Mark O. Haroldsen

Library of Congress Control Number: 2007940594

Published and distributed in the United States by:
The Leading Edge Publishing Company
PO Box 7411
Waco, TX 76714
www.theleadingedgepublishing.com

Printed in the United States of America

ISBN: 978-0-89811-552-9 (paperback version)
ISBN 13: 978-0-89811-553-6 (hardback version)

Contents

Addendums

Acknowledgments & Special Thanks

There are so many people to thank—I simply cannot list all of those who have helped me and influenced my life. That would be a separate book by itself. But I would like to acknowledge and give special thanks to those people who have helped and influenced me and have given me suggestions and encouragement in writing this particular book.

First of all, I'd like to thank **Marina Miles** for her enthusiastic acceptance of the words I wrote, which encouraged me to write even more. She is an incredible person who adds so very much to the world. **Mike Hansen** deserves so much credit I can hardly put it into words. Yes, he brought the whole project together and without him it never would have happened. But there is so much more! He was bold enough to challenge my opinions and some of my conclusions, especially when it came to the end of the book and my "God thoughts" that didn't square with his. He has the wonderful ability to gently guide people toward smart decisions without banging them over the head. This is truly a rare quality. He is one of the most giving people on the planet. People like Mike Hansen make me believe that there may be a God. I sure hope so—or as someone once said that only a fool would hope there is no God and another life for us all. Without Marina and Mike, this book would not exist.

And now I acknowledge and thank . . . you, the reader for taking the time to read and examine my thoughts. I hope that my little book will enhance your life to the MAX . . . that is my very sincere wish.

I also thank and acknowledge my wonderful wife, **Kimberly**, who has been so very loving and supportive and has been a good sounding board for my ideas . . . even when they were a bit weird. Coming from a huge family with such great parents (**Ted and Karen Carton**—from the itty-bitty town of Grants Pass, Oregon), Kimberly learned at a young age how to share and give, she does that every day of her life—my thanks to Ted and Karen for being such super parents.

Next, I would like to thank my children—**Mark Ed, David, Nichol, Camille, Marcus, George, and Lindsey**, who were not afraid to give me great input and sometimes even say, "Dad, that's a real stupid idea . . ."

when such comments were appropriate. Each one of them has turned into truly super-responsible young adults that contribute so much to the world. They are a great testimony to the faithful, consistent love and hard work of their mothers: **Lois Ann Haroldsen, Karen Boswell Johnson**, and **Kelly Hansen Packe**r.

Special thanks go to **Paul J. Meyer** for giving me his time unselfishly and his ideas and input . . . and to others who have been particularly helpful with this project: **Radd Berrett, Mike and Ileana Delaney, Richard Harvey** (my soul brother to the end), **Ed Beckham** (my non-blood big brother). Also my good friends, **Dr. Craig Davis, William A. King** (aka WAK), **Dennis Johnson, Brittany Peters** (for putting up with me all this time),and **George Winquist** (one of the most superb listeners I've ever met) with whom I have shared half a lifetime. We both have, very sadly, lost a child in the prime of their lives. And finally, I sincerely acknowledge and thank **Seldon Young** for his great inspiration, **Jerry and Judy Higginson** for their help in coming up with the title for this book, and **David Craig** for his timely and unedited feedback.

Foreword

Have you ever noticed that many times in life it takes a great tragedy to wake a person up so he or she starts grasping virtually every moment that life has to offer and start living passionately?

**I think it can safely be said that to live life
without real passion is to not have fully lived.**

Most of us, at one time or another, have experienced the great feeling of living with great passion, only to have it dissipate a short time later. The real trick is to squeeze out every bit of passion in living for our entire lives.

- **So how do we ignite or reignite our passion for living so it stays with us?**

- **Can we learn this lesson without having to suffer through a huge and catastrophic event?**

- **Is there a way—a method or a formula to keep us from wasting a single moment or a single breath?**

The answer to these questions, I believe, is an unqualified, **"Yes."** There is a way—there are answers—and actually some of those answers to these critically important questions you already know.

There's a fantastic Zen saying:

To know and not to do, is not yet to know.

In other words, some of what I'm going to tell you in this book you already know. I'm fully aware that as you read this book, you may say to yourself many times, "I know about this" or "Hey, does this author think I'm slow, stupid, or what?" or "I already know how this stuff works."

Please understand. What I'm saying as loud as I can say, again, is:

To know and not to do, is not yet to know.

So if you're not doing, you're really not knowing. And it is absolutely obvious that most people are not doing it or there would be so many more people whose lives were full of passion, achievement, health, wealth, and contentment.

Let me show you how to really do it and ignite your PASSION for living—and lift your achievement and contentment factor in the health and wealth department of your life to a whole new level.

That is, if you will let me. It will take the two of us to make this work. My best advice to you is to read this book with pen in hand. Write down your thoughts as you go. Write in the margins of this book. Underline and circle the things that grab you and those things that can particularly help you. Write down your own "to do" list.

I know without question that the concepts, principles, and keys that I've written about have worked for me and have greatly enhanced my life—especially the second half of my life—and can do the same for you and for those you love and care about and to whom you pass on this book.

I've given my all in writing this—I've held nothing back. I am absolutely driven, and passionately so, to greatly enhance your life. I believe very strongly that what is contained in this book can and will do that. There really are some secrets contained in these pages that will push you and keep you in the "mental Zen state" of knowing and also of doing.

Years ago when I started writing my first book, friends, family, and even strangers all had their opinions. Some were very strong opinions as to if I should write it or not. I also had my own doubts. Would it help anyone? Would anyone buy it? Well, 2,000,000 people bought *How To Wake Up The Financial Genius Inside You*. I have been so very gratified by the thousands of individuals who have taken time to personally contact me and share with me how the book has catapulted them on to great wealth in their own lives (over a billion dollars in one instance).

And so with this book, my intent is very clear:

To speed you along on a wildly exciting quest to live life more fully—to live it with great PASSION and PURPOSE—and to turn your deepest DREAMS into REALITY. Let's begin, NOW!

SPECIAL NOTE TO EACH READER

Squeezing *The Most You Can* From This Book

The Awesome Power of Spaced Repetition

Would you believe there is a 41-year-old woman from California who can remember almost every single day of her life since age 11? Give her any date in the last 30 years and she can tell you where she went and what she did (according to the November 2007 issue of *National Geographic* magazine).

Unfortunately, I don't have a brain that works like that. Most likely, you don't either. However, there is something we can do that will pay huge dividends in each of our lives.

It's called learning and remembering from **spaced repetition**. The concept is simple. It's one I learned years ago from one of my favorite people, Paul J. Meyer. His advice was:

*"Rather than read a thousand different books, **find a few** that are powerful and life-changing and read them **many times**. Wait between readings for the material to sift through your brain, and then read the book again. With the repetition, you'll remember more of the information and more of what you learn will really sink in."*

So Here's My Challenge To You

If this book is a powerful force for you, truly helpful, uplifting, and life-enhancing the first time through it—GREAT! Now read it again—and again.

Spaced repetition is the mother of all **learning**. Actually DOING what you learn is the proven path to RETENTION and creating the RESULTS you most desire—and the way to get what you really (I mean REALLY) WANT.

CHAPTER ONE

Return to Exuberance

There may be nothing that fires up the mind, puts a spring in your step, or enhances your whole life quite like accomplishing something BIG. To enthusiastically pursue something that's EXCITING to you, that you've thought long and hard about—**even dreamed about**—is a sure-fire way to feel wonderfully alive and passionate about living.

And the beauty of it all, is to feel this way, **it doesn't matter how old you are—you can be a young buck or an old fart.**

However ...

**sometimes the young may lack the courage
to go for something BIG**

or

**they may doubt they have enough experience
or knowledge or resources
to make it happen.**

And those who are older ...

**sometimes fall into the thinking trap
that it's too late—that somehow
they've run out of time.**

A tragic thing can happen to your life as you're on the way to your death. What some call a "midlife crisis" hits hard.

1

What happens? You begin to ...

run out of steam,
stagnate,
lose confidence,
trust in yourself, and
even give up on life.

Many Die Inside, Long Before They're Buried

Make no mistake, even young folks can experience this! There are too many in their 30s and younger who *quit on themselves* and *never reach their full potential*.

Others think they have *all the time in the world* and never quite *grab hold of their lives* or *find direction and true purpose*.

You see evidence of this "crisis" everywhere,
among all age groups.

You can hear it in the way people talk about their lives
and about the future.

You can see it in their eyes when you really
pay attention to people.

Listen to their unenthusiastic or cynical voices and
what they are talking about.

Watch how they walk.

Look at the many oversized bodies.

What has happened to them? Aren't we well-educated in this country? Isn't there a lot of wealth and opportunity all around? Why are so many people beginning to die just when they are in a position to be having the time of their life?

Future View

When we were children, the future looked bright, inviting, and full of possibilities. We could hardly wait to embrace it and we set our young sights on becoming an astronaut or Miss America or racing horses or driving a racecar or getting rich or traveling the world.

> As children, we faced limit-less possibilities ... but we aged and the possibilites became limited. WHAT HAPPENED?

But somehow, between then and the midlife of now, we lose our way. We lose sight of our dreams. We become more "practical" when it comes to the day-to-day. We even lose hope for a better future.

Why is that? More importantly, *how did it happen?*

Why do so many people just let go of life and let themselves go— **physically, mentally, financially, and in so many other ways?**

When Life Speeds Up, Many Slow Down

What, then, is the answer—the solution? It's right there in the corner of your mind.

It's all about death.

Whose death?

YOUR DEATH!

It's all about how your mind begins to think about your own inevitable demise, your checkout time, your *adios amigos* day—or in other words, the end. YOUR end.

As you and I hit midlife and beyond, we can't help but begin thinking of our lives in a totally different way than we did when we were 18, 25, or even 35. Back then we intellectually knew that someday we were going to die. But on a real *gut level*, or on an *emotional level*, we really couldn't ac-cept or believe this about ourselves. That event was so far in the future that it wasn't real to us.

But at 40 or 50, and especially at 60, we know for sure that our days are numbered and we sense that time is speeding up dramatically.

So what happens in our brains when we come to that realization? What happens in those few inches between our ears?

Do you find yourself thinking, "Why challenge myself? Why set goals? Why lose weight and get in great physical shape? Why change careers? Why make more money? Why write a book?"

Turn the Clock Back, Now

It doesn't have to be that way! The first step is to admit it. Has this negative, life-has-passed-me-by, it's-too-late-for-me thinking got in your head?

**NOW, choose in this moment to commit
to a totally different mental course for yourself.**

**COMMIT to a new course filled with hope, excitement,
accomplishment, ultimate health, and a long life.**

I believe you can turn the clock back and embrace all the wonderful possibilities that exist all around us—*like you used to do everyday as a kid*.

This is more than positive thinking ... **this is very active possibility thinking and magnificent possibility living.**

Try Out a New Possibility, Right Now

Start now by setting a goal, and (this is VERY important) write it down on paper, **"I'm going to live an additional 60 healthy years."**

Yes, you read that right: *an additional 60 years!* Set that goal even if you're 50 years old, right now! (You will read more later about how you have an excellent shot at really doing that.)

If you can really "buy into" your new overall goal of living a longer and healthier life, **you're going to have a lot more time to achieve many of your dreams—*more than you EVER thought possible!***

If an 18- or 20-year-old can set goals and achieve them, then you, as an older and wiser person filled with years of experience and life's lessons, have a **huge advantage** and a **much greater likelihood of success.**

4

However ...

when you don't have your own goals and objectives for your life firmly set,

and

you don't have your own blueprint,

then

just about any idea is likely to sweep you away.

If you don't have your own clearly thought-out, well-defined course, you may easily be persuaded to follow someone else's dream or plan.

Many people just **drift along** and let other people or situations dictate what will happen in their lives. They often **spend their days** reacting to situations and to other people **without taking charge** of their own lives and deciding where they want to go.

> **You can turn the clock back and embrace all the wonderful possibilities that exist all around you ... like you used to everyday!**

Consequently, when they look at their lives and realize they haven't achieved what they had hoped for or dreamed about, they ...

- **begin to lose trust in themselves,**
- **blame themselves,**
- **think they're somehow inadequate,**
- **believe they have no power over their own lives.**

At that point, they certainly don't believe goal setting will work. Their reasoning is simple: **"Goal setting has never worked for me before, so why should it now?"**

Of course, what's really happening is that they **never have set any well-thought-out, clearly defined, written goals** with specific time frames to achieve them.

5

Essential Direction

Also, most people on this planet tend to be **outwardly** directed instead of being **inwardly** directed when it comes to taking charge of their own lives.

Some of us were very inwardly directed when we were young, but lost much of it by midlife as we become outwardly directed.

Many allow the job, obligations, duties, responsibilities, and all the "have-to" things that become part of day-to-day life to monopolize their time. There's always something to do for someone else. **That's a good thing, right?**

Maybe not if in all our "doing" we only respond to others and not to what lies deep inside us.

To be inwardly directed, we are able to do with our lives exactly what we want to do. This is not to say that we ignore others or ignore our obligations or duties and just blissfully dance to our own whims and desires. No.

Do you want to have more, do more, and be more?

To be inwardly directed is to be true to what lives for us in our minds, hearts, and souls.

Honestly, are you true to what you aspire to HAVE, to DO, and to BE?

I believe *the vast majority of human beings* just kind of bump along with the crowd, adhering to what others prescribe for them, with no goals or dreams of their own, just existing or living average lives until they die.

That's okay, of course, if that's what they really want ... **but I think most people want so much more!**

Return to Exuberance

I promise you that you can get back that fantastic feeling you had as a kid when life was exciting and you lived fully—**when you went at life full throttle, with great passion, glee, and enthusiasm.**

That child-like exuberance can come flowing back into your life the *INSTANT* you go for a dream—something that is living inside of you, that's not on the outside, yet.

I'm sure once in a while you meet or see people who are way past their prime ... **who are in high passion mode!** Most of the time you are impressed and in awe of them.

However ...

if you're like most people, you quickly dismiss them because of jealously born from your ego.

But if you and I are really paying attention and keep our ego out of it, we can realize and see how we have fallen short somehow of our own potential. If we realize this, then, and only then, can we begin to change ourselves and learn from those we see putting themselves back into the high passion mode.

Let me emphasize a very key ingredient to igniting **GREAT PASSION**—here it is: Your dreams or goals or personal challenges have to be BIG, even difficult.

Why?

Because they must have power to
***stir* you, *inspire* you, *awe* you,**
***excite* you, and maybe even**
***frighten* you a little.**

And amazingly, as you BEGIN to struggle, work, and sweat toward a difficult and exciting objective, I promise you that an unmistakable youthful exuberance for life will overtake you, even before you achieve the objective.

Why? **Because you are NOW fully engaged in life.** In fact, you are passionate about it rather than just being a stoic, uninspired bystander.

What I Know

What the majority of people (young and old) don't know is this: **There is a way to reach virtually every goal you'll ever set!**

And I'm going to try every way I know how, as a writer and a practitioner, to show you and prove to you that you can reach any goal you set.

To set a goal and reach it can make the difference:

between super wealth ... and poverty;
between excellence ... and mediocrity;
between great, long-lasting health ... and illness; and
between life ... and death.

But the million-dollar question is: **How can you be successful and reach your goals every time you set them?**

Sure-Fire Success

Is there a secret formula? Is there a sure-fire path you can follow to ensure that you reach each goal every time you set one? The answer is an emphatic **"YES!"**

I'll show you exactly how this is done.

I know you can do it.

I know this because I've done it.

And more importantly, I've helped and showed literally tens of thousand of others how to do it.

But there are some "secrets" or shortcuts to success that you need to learn and you *will learn* by reading this book.

Here's One of Those Valuable "Secrets"

All of us make decisions that guide our lives for good or bad. That's a given.

What you and I must understand and set firmly in our brains is this:

BEFORE any future events or situations come up, it is our goals that will drive every decision that we will make in relation to those future events or situations.

The problem is, that most of the time, **we haven't** really made that clear decision beforehand. **We haven't** firmly and clearly set out a specific goal of where we are going and what we want to be doing.

We haven't set our minds!

Consequently, we may lack that critically important "mindset" to direct or guide a particular part of our lives, whether it relates to our finances, our weight, our health, our self-improvement, or whatever.

Let me give you two specifics of what I'm talking about:

1. **FINANCIAL:** You've set your mind on a specific financial goal — let's say to make $200,000 in the next 18 months. You've mapped out a plan that requires a few thousand dollars of "seed money" to get started—and you've got just the right amount of that seed money in your bank account. If you've gone that far and you have really set your mind on that goal, then when a great buy on a car, boat, cruise, vacation, clothes, a night out on the town, or any other buying "opportunity" pops up, and you've already set your mind (I mean firmly), then those so-called "opportunities" that arise won't even begin to tempt you. You've already made the decision where that money is going! You will not struggle or have to reason out or rationalize what to do, because your mind has already been firmly set. That's why it's called a mindset!

2. **HEALTH:** Let's say you've set your mind firmly on a goal to lose exactly 25 pounds and really get in shape (and this time keep the weight off). You already know how critically important it is to be healthy. After all, who wants to have a few million dollars, a great lifestyle, and a lot of success and then die of a preventable disease at age 45 or 55? Who wants to be in a situation where you're financially comfortable but not able to get off the couch, let alone move easily, run, play, go cycling, or whatever you enjoy doing? With a firm goal set in your mind and written down with a timeframe, you will be prepared to resist the temptations that will inevitably assail you. If you want a delicious piece of strawberry cheesecake, or you walk into a Target Superstore and see a huge display of mouth-watering Krispy Kreme donuts, you will easily be able to say "No!" because you've already made that decision beforehand. No mind debate—no rationalizing —no mental hassle—is required. It's not even an open-and-shut matter, because you never opened it in the first place!

> **Do your goals drive every decision you make in relation to those future events or situations?**

Creating Your Own Wake-Up Call

Even a simple thing works, like making a decision the night before regarding how you're going to react when your alarm goes off the next morning. **Believe me, I know from many years of experience on this one!**

If I don't make a decision the night before, I will wake up and lay in bed playing stupid mind games, debating internally, and making up reasons why I really don't need to get up right then.

On the other hand, if I have set my mind the night before, I get out of bed immediately upon waking with a specific plan of attack: 5 minutes in the hot tub as I watch the news, followed by a shower, and a cup of coffee while I dress. Then I'm off and running, and I have avoided all that negative stuff and the energy-sucking mind debates.

By the way, with whom are we debating when we do that mind debate? **Are there really two of us inside of our heads?**

Actually, there really are two. Call that "second-self" your alter ego, your subconscious or your other brain—I don't care what you call it, but it's there. As you will see later, **you can make your second self your ally and partner, or allow it to continue to be your enemy.**

It's your choice to use this incredible power or not—*you need to be of one mind*—not two!

Don't Trade What You Want Most for What May Be Tantalizing You Now

Again, if you really want more from life, then you must firmly and precisely set your mind not only on your objective and your goal, but— *this is critical*—also on exactly what you're going to do in all those (as many as you can identify) daily or weekly or monthly situations along the way that tempt you to put off or trade what you REALLY WANT for what may be enticing you right now.

**Those current temptations,
even perhaps tantalizing,
most likely have little or no long-lasting value.**

Decide beforehand, and then you will automatically know how to respond before something happens.

When your mind is firmly set, well in advance, **then you won't hesitate for even a moment or try to rationalize any other response other than the one that pushes you closer to your ultimate goal.**

If this magic key called a **mindset** is in cement in your head and heart, then the likelihood of your triumph is greatly enhanced—almost assured.

> **Temptations have no power when you are 100% focused on reaching your goal?**

That little insight was just to get the ball rolling. (See more in Chapter Nine) I hope you enjoy it and use it.

It really does work!

Proven Success Formula

The pages that follow will give you the formulas for **financial**, **family** and **physical** health, and *success for any type of goal you choose to pursue ... and much more.*

Specifically, you will learn how to **super-charge** your ability to reach all your goals by using the power of B-RAM™ lists with all your goals.

This alone could virtually guarantee that you won't give up or become sidelined as you go after your goals.

You will also be given some critical keys that add a huge dose of satisfaction and contentment to your life. (**Please note, I didn't say "happiness."**) I firmly believe that to pursue a goal of happiness is folly. Happiness is and should be a by-product of achieving your goals, as I think you will see and experience.

Plus, I think you will also see that **satisfaction and contentment are far superior and longer-lasting feelings than so-called happiness.**

And this brings us to *PASSION*—true passion for life, why it's so important, and why we shouldn't live a day without it.

CHAPTER TWO

Short *Life* Needs *BIG* Passion

L ife is too darn short to live without passion.

Time squandered is wasted—gone forever.

Don't be like those who,
later in life, realize that they missed
out on so many opportunities.

I believe most people, when looking back at their lives, are in more pain over the things they didn't do than over the things they failed at while trying to do them.

We receive long-lasting benefit,
and yes, even deep satisfaction from working hard
and giving something worthwhile, our all.

Passion: Head and Shoulders Over Pleasure

There are many who think the way to achieve satisfaction in life is by going after pleasure. They think that more and more pleasure will put more contentment in their lives.

Sorry, it doesn't work that way.

There's a huge difference between deep,
enduring satisfaction and fleeting
pleasure—between passion and a good time.

At a gut level you already know this. The pursuit of pleasure for its own sake leads to misery.

It's also not easy to always remain at a high level of satisfaction and contentment with an effervescent passion for life. There are plenty of setbacks. Even at times, huge fists of adversity may pound us in the face.

These setbacks and adversity often reveal to us the great lessons of life, if we will just learn from them.

I've certainly had my share of setbacks, even tragedies. I wouldn't choose to be faced with these tragedies, I must say that since they did happen, they served as huge life lessons and wake-up calls that I don't think I could have learned any other way.

Let me briefly share some of my stories.

Sudden-Death Wake-Up Call

I was the second-born in my family. I was always trying to measure up to my older brother. We were close in age and also close competitors. We went hard at everything, including one of our shared passions—basketball. We were on the same team together. I was always eager to prove that I belonged on the court with him.

Then one day, in an **INSTANT**,
**my whole life was forever changed at the age of 15,
when I became the oldest child in the family.**

My older brother died, literally at my feet, while we were playing a basketball game in an outdoor stadium in the middle-eastern country of Turkey, I was devastated. It happened just six weeks after our family had pulled up stakes and moved half-way around the world. (I visited that very same stadium in downtown Ankara, Turkey almost 50 years later.) The moment of my

> **One shattering event forced me to confront the hard reality that life is fragile and the time we have has undeniable, precious value.**

brother's death remains burned into my mind. I can remember it vividly even as I write these words.

That one, shattering event permanently altered how I look at life.

It forced me to confront the hard reality that life is fragile, it can be very short, and it can end in an unexpected moment. I now knew that reality.

Knowing that can be both a great blessing and a curse. However, that early event was a dramatic wake-up call for me—one that has driven me ever since to do more—much more with my life than I otherwise would have. **From that moment, I've always had an acute sense of time and its undeniable, precious value.**

Also, I became very motivated by my brother's death to play basketball at a much higher level.

This passion became a goal to play professional basketball. In my 15-year-old brain I figured out that if I became a great basketball player that somehow my brother would be able to "live" through me—making up for his early death.

Here I am (front, left) with my Ankara (Turkey) high school basketball team, as we emerge triumphantly from the plane. We had just been crowned 1961 High School Mediterranean Champions having won the tournament in Rome. Next to me is Steve Switzer. Next row is Whit Campbell and Richard Harvey. In back is Ed Beckcom and Henry Carey.

However, there was a problem.

I had a **great goal** without a **great plan.**

Oh yes, I had PASSION for basketball, BUT what I didn't realize then was that although passion is critical, there is so much more to a winning formula to reach a GREAT GOAL.

How to Run Out of Gas

Today, I like to tell people, "Yes, I played basketball for Utah State University." But then I slowly admit that I had a great seat on the bench to watch the games.

I made the university team, mostly because of my hustle and a good resume. My high school team had won the overseas high school championship in Rome, Italy. And, of course, I had dedicated my performance that season and the championship to my brother. And that passionate, personal performance helped get me to the next level.

But then came the lesson. **I learned that PASSION is to LIFE as high-octane gas is to a Lamborghini.** With its tank full, the Lamborghini can run fast and far. But with no specific direction or timeframe to get to a destination—even a Lamborghini will eventually run out of gas.

That's what happened to me.

As I sat at the end of the bench, my dream to be the next Bob Cousy started to fade. (If you don't know who Bob Cousy was—think Michael Jordan.)

As I look back, it was inevitable:

- **I didn't have a well thought-out plan to reach my goal.**

- **I had no high-level, skill development program in my workouts.**

- **I hadn't attached time frames or targets to my development. I hadn't spent extra time with coaches or other successful players working on my game. I didn't have an ultra-conditioning program.**

- **I had very little dedication to my training, especially during the off-season.**

■ **I had no real game plan on how to get to the NBA. I was just driving around—even driving fast and hard, but ultmately— "I ran out of gas."**

However, as I look back this was not a setback. It was really a very crucial life lesson.

A Million Dollar Goal

I began to formulate a new GOAL. But this time, it wasn't about basketball. And my goal was not unusual at the time. In fact, I think most people (at least in the United States) contemplate this particular goal at least once in their life: The goal to make a million dollars.

> **Believe it or not, almost every**
> **"middle American family"**
> **actually succeeds in making a**
> **million dollars—even a bit more.**

The only drawback is that it takes 30 years or so for the average wage earner to make a million. (It takes a little more than $33,000 a year income to equal a million dollars in total earnings over 30 years, the majority of which is spent along the way.)

That wasn't what I was thinking.

I wanted to make a cool million (and by that I mean a net worth of a million dollars). **I wanted it so much I could taste it. My passion was rising.**

After college, I moved to Denver, Colorado, and I went to work for a large stock brokerage company.

Learning from my basketball shortfall, this time I closely observed what wealthy individuals did to become wealthy.

■ **I boldly interviewed them.**

■ **I studied their lives.**

- ■ I devoured books and information of all kinds on making money.

- ■ I saved and got smart people to coach me.

- ■ Then I implemented a very valuable part of the goal-setting formula.

A Deadline

By the time I was 30 years old I would be a millionaire. That was my time frame. I was 27 at the time. Of course, putting an absolute time limit or deadline on every goal is an indispensable part of the formula.

> **Putting an absolute time limit or deadline on every goal is an indispensable part of the formula.**

That's probably why so many people who say they want to make a million dollars actually end up making a million dollars, but they never put a time frame on it. So they succeed, at least in a manner of speaking—it just takes them 30 years and most of it is spent along the way!

Certainly setting the goal and putting a time frame on it is not all you have to do to achieve a goal, as you will see later in this book, but it is a fantastic and valuable start.

> **But you can tell by my time frame that I was in a hurry to**
>
> **become a millionaire. Life was so short in my mind,**
>
> **and I knew from experience that sobering and scary fact.**

Had I known some of the other parts of the formula, which I discovered later, I'm certain that I would have succeeded right on time. My first million dollars (net worth) came just one year late, at age 31. Now that first million dollars has multiplied many times over, but so has something else—something more valuable for me than the money.

What Money Is and Is Not

Almost everybody (if they're honest) wants money—and usually, they would prefer a lot of it. Many see money as a path to happiness. Well, maybe not.

Philip Brickman, a sociologist at Northwest University did a survey of lottery players in the State of Illinois, interviewing both the winners and losers. Much to some people's surprise, he found that the winners were no happier than the people who played the lottery and lost. Remarkable.

According to Gregory Berns, MD, PhD, in his very insightful book called *Satisfaction: The Science Of Finding True Fulfillment*, Berns shares this:

> **"If money does not buy the right to avoid decisions, it does something even better—it buys you possibilities. The higher up the income ladder you go, the more things become possible."**

Berns goes on to say,

> **"Conventional economic wisdom would suggest that money is only as good as what you can turn it into."**

Accruing Possibilities

When you build up a supply of money, you're actually accruing possibilities and not just the material goods it can buy—you accrue ways to improve your own life and the lives of those around you, satisfy needs, and to provide a platform from which you can make the world a better place, as well.

Perhaps that sounds like a way to personal peace and contentment.

Right?

Well, still some questions linger when we hear about the lives of many wealthy philanthropists who do not feel personally fulfilled or content, despite their generous and effective giving.

"The question on my mind is not what most people do with money," Dr. Berns continues,

> **"but why money doesn't lead to lasting improvement and well-being for most people. The answer lies in what you do to get money."**

The bottom line then is that it's really the **"journey"** to accrue possibilities that brings you lasting satisfaction. It's the work and effort along the way that is the real key to fulfillment—not just the money.

I also have found that to be very true. Money does open up possibilities, but if you don't enjoy the journey, you've missed the point. It's the love of and passion for the journey that makes it so fulfilling.

Beyond Money

I think one reason so much is said and written about goal setting being attached to a money outcome is because **it's easy to measure your progress when you have something that can be quantified by numbers**.

When you have a goal to improve the parts of your life that are non-financial, you'll see that **it's a bit tougher to measure such as:**

■ spiritual,

■ family,

■ friends,

■ social,

■ health,

■ or a personal goal like overcoming fear.

But these non-financial goals can also be achieved following the same basic path and formula.

> **I wanted to make a ton of money so I could pursue other dreams that would benefit and include my family every step of the way while making a difference in people's lives.**

In my case I really wanted to make a ton of money so I could then pursue other dreams—dreams like world travel, living in exotic places, benefiting from having my family with me every step of the way, and making a huge difference in people's lives. (For more on money, see Addendum A: Winning the Money Game—Without Being Devoured By It.)

Money and the Good It Can Do

One last thought about money. Don't dismiss money as "the root of all evil"—thinking you were quoting the Bible, because the Bible doesn't say that.

It says the root of all evil is the love of money, not the money itself. Money can be absolutely the most "non-love" wonderful thing in the world. It can:

■ **Save lives,**

■ **Provide heart transplants,**

■ **Build schools and hospitals for poor people,**

■ **Rebuild homes for earthquake and tsunami victims,**

and it can give:

■ **Peace of mind and enhance a sense of security in anyone's life.**

Therefore, money and the good it can do should be a non-apologetic part of your dreams.

Where Are You Headed?

Where, then, do you want your life to head?

Where and what do you want to experience and become along the way?

Even if you are at midlife now and experiencing some "crisis" and do not know for sure exactly what you want—that's okay. I think that's quite normal, in fact.

I've not always known exactly where I was going—and I must admit—at times I think and ponder for months or even years about just what dreams I want to shift from my "dream list" to my "goal list."

> **Life is short so we need to live our lives with all the PASSION AND PURPOSE possible!**

And, as you will begin to see more clearly, that's a very important part of the whole process.

One Ounce of Excitement

Yes, your life and my life, they're short so we need to live these lives with all the PASSION and PURPOSE possible—to savor every moment.

The character of Bill Parrish, played by Anthony Hopkins in the movie *Meet Joe Black*, says it so well with what he called "Parrish by-words." He said that he was ***always looking for that one ounce of excitement, that whisper of a thrill that makes no sense of living your life without.***

Now this next question is important.

> **It is central to living life on your terms**
> **and in a state of excitement—**
> **doing that which makes life thrilling,**
> **even with all its ups and downs.**

The answer to this question is the common ground we must both be standing on in order for us to move forward.

If it's not clear yet, then let's ask it:

Why should you or I or anybody set goals, anyway?

Let's move on to Chapter Three, for a deeper look.

CHAPTER THREE

Why Set Goals Anyway?

What if I were to tell you that over and above all the success, material benefit, satisfaction, and even wealth that you could receive from achieving a very exciting goal, that you can dramatically improve your emotional and mental health by just the process of setting that goal in the first place.

Now, that's quite a promise—

and believe me, I'm not making it lightly.

Years ago I noticed that when I became engrossed in my goal-setting state of mind (almost a meditative state), I would begin to feel very calm and at peace with the world—even euphoric, and almost always with pen in hand, I wrote down all that was going on in my mind and heart.

I didn't understand why it felt so good—so fantastic, in fact—I just knew it did.

Of course, it was a wonderful triumph to actually reach or exceed the goals I set, but I couldn't figure out why just the **process of thinking about and writing my goals and plans** gave me such a mental boost.

> **You can dramatically improve your emotional and mental health by the process of setting a goal.**

The Dalai Lama's Request

I found an explanation of why this could be so in *Time* magazine, of all places. A University of Wisconsin professor, Richard Davidson, who *Time* magazine had honored as one of the "100 People Who Shape Our World," was actually asked by the Dalai Lama to study the connection between the meditative state of mind of his Buddhist monks and their emotional and mental health.

Davidson first hooked 128 electrodes to the head of a French-born monk, Mattieu Ricard, and recorded an immediate increase in the gamma activity when the monk began to meditate. Later studies with a control group showed that "monks produce gamma waves that were 30 times stronger than the control group."

But what does all this mean? Simply put, this and other research unveils the real possibility that the brain, like the rest of the body, can be altered intentionally.

Just as we build muscle through exercise,

we can also build our mental capacities that can lead

to better brain function and an increase in essential cognitive

functions, including memory and perception.

This all creates a more positive mental state—and that's what in turn creates more productive gamma brain waves. But there's more.

Changing Gray Matter

Davidson actually found that "meditation results in a redistribution of gray matter in the brain and thwarts decline in the loss of gray matter." According to Davidson,

> **"Meditation might also be used to modify maladaptive emotional responses, like depression."**

Antidote for Depression?

Well, that leads to this question:

> **"Could my own thinking about and setting goals**
> **and then figuring out how to fulfill them**
> **keep me from being depressed?"**

To that, I answer a resounding "YES!"

I base that on proof from my own personal experience and financial results.

I also credit my "rosy" outlook on the whole of my life to my regular goal setting sessions, where I ponder intently:

- **Where I'm going with my life,**

- **Review the results so far,**

- **Adjust and tweak,**

- **And set new goals or revise existing plans based on feedback or new information or new opportunities.**

Now, let me be clear. Passionate goal setting and pursuing those goals with enthusiasm and a firm mindset certainly do chase the clouds away for me. And they can also bring me out of a good case of the blues. I've experienced that time and time again.

But all depression is not the same for all.

There are those individuals who suffer from clinical depression. There are a host of reasons for this condition. Those who experience clinical depression:

- **Often suffer severe sorrow and even suicidal thoughts.**

- **They may act irrationally and become forgetful.**

- **No matter what, they can't seem to climb out of a big hole in which they find themselves.**

Brain chemical imbalances can be a major part of clinical depression, but can usually be managed through medication. One simple fix for many men, especially over age 60, can be a topical testosterone gel (for those whose testosterone is low as shown by a simple blood test).

Goal setting may not be part of a prescription program—but I believe strongly that it may certainly play a supportive role on the road to recovery.

Additionally, the brain's reaction to refined and processed foods

> It's difficult to get down and dwell on what's going wrong when you are creating such good mental and physical energy from positive goal setting!

has been linked to feelings of depression. I've experienced this myself after a sugar binge or when I've been on a high-protein diet. However, this diet-induced depression for me usually disappeared with better nutrition and exercise. (Read more later on in this book about diet and the critical factor it is to longevity and success in Chapter 10, "An Umbrella Goal for LIFE.")

Now remember this.

It's difficult to get down and dwell on what's going wrong when you are creating such good mental and physical energy from positive, productive goal setting.

Goals and the Energy They Create

Want more proof that a goal can create physical energy, too? Try this: If you have young kids, or grandkids, walk into a room where they're watching television (the great energy draining machine) and say,

> **"Hey kids, who would like to go out to the airport right now and jump on a plane and fly to Walt Disney World?"**

You'll see how fast energy can be created in kids who were sitting without hardly any energy just seconds before.

Such is the power of a tantalizing goal!

The words you spoke to your kids are just sounds, but those sounds communicated a thought that brings a visual picture in your kids mind. They can quickly "see" themselves at Walt Disney World and just from those brain images comes excitement and energy—even passion.

Wow!

All that from just sounds that came out of your mouth!

Our Own Adrenaline Rush

Of course, all of us understand the physical energy that comes in a blinding flash of mortal danger. If you're suddenly confronted by a grizzly bear on a mountain trail, most likely you will instantly feel a huge surge of energy—and be able to run faster and farther than you ever have before or even thought possible for you.

You can also create your own adrenaline rush

when you become committed and motivated to

reach a deadline that you've set—and really want to meet!

I've done this with my BIG exciting goals:

■ **First, I make up my mind that nothing will stand in my way.**

■ **Second, I push myself, days at a time, with little rest, and remarkably without exhaustion to accomplish my goal. (Compare that with how tired you may get when you're doing something you don't want to do, after just an hour?)**

Up to a Higher Level

Am I saying then, that if you spend time setting goals that you could nearly eliminate depression from your life, and your mental, emotional, and physical health will improve?

Well, I believe that—but it depends on your unique self.

It depends if you seriously spend enough intense time setting specific, powerful **GOALS** that **excite** and **inspire** you. And then by working intently on those goals (as I will show you how to do in this book), I truly believe you will greatly enhance

your mind,

    your health,

        your outlook on life,

            and be able to live at a new and higher level.

I believe that, because it has happened in my life, and I've personally seen it happen in the lives of thousands upon thousands of others.

> **The most important point is that goalsetting works for you!**

If you experience that for yourself, then who cares if all this new-found enhancement and success in your life was the result of technical stuff like increased brain gamma waves or neurons responding to new events or adrenaline or whatever—**the most important point is that goalsetting just simply works—for you!**

Goals Are the Mirror of What You Really Want—So Write Them Down

Remember this:

Goals are a true reflection of what you

want out of life—put into action.

Start by sincerely and intently asking yourself, "What do I really (I MEAN REALLY) want out of life?"

Be honest with what you really want—and this is important—write it down, don't just think about it. What are your dreams? Write them down. What are your deeply held desires and the "Oh-I-wish-I-could-do-that" things that live in your heart?

Some of those "things" you've never told a soul about—those "things" that just send a shiver of delight though you as you think about them. Write them down.

Are you getting the point here?
Why all this about writing things down?

This is a very crucial part, I believe, of getting where you want to go. Putting your thoughts, dreams, wants, and GOALS down on paper, brings them into existence.

They are no longer just hidden away in your brain as impulses or wishes.

Writing down your wants, your dreams, and your goals gives them a tangible presence in this world.

Writing them down:

- **shapes them,**

- **gives them expression,**

- **form, and clarity.**

It gives them handles so you can carry them with you, to remind, to inspire, to motivate, and get you going in the direction you define.

> **Rereading them often—even every day—makes**
> **them a part of you and harder for you to**
> **rationalize them away or wimp out.**

The goals that you set (and write down) with specific time frames and plans to achieve them to them are true reflections of what you really want. (See more on writing-things-down in Chapter Five, "Turning Your Dreams into Reality.")

Be Equal to Your Gains and Gifts

And don't forget while you're writing about what you want your life to be like, be careful that you don't leave out this:

- **What you want to become along the way.**

- **What kind of person do you want to be—what attributes and characteristics do you want to pull into your life to make your own?**

Rarely will a person "get or give a lot" from life without being equal as a person to their gains or gifts along the way.

Knowing what you really want combined with what you really want to become, can truly supercharge you and push you beyond what you ever thought was possible—and to do things you never dreamed you could do.

So Why Would You Want to Cut Off Your Own Arm?

Want to measure how important and powerful identifying what you really want can be to your life? Now stick with me. There's a very important point you will soon see by asking this question:

Would you cut off your arm for $10,000?

(And I mean cut it off with a small knife,

without any drugs or anesthetic.)

Is your answer, No?

Well, how about for $100,000? Would that make you want to do it? Or would it take $1,000,000 to motivate you to do something that drastic?

Money can be a powerful motivator,

but for me and probably for most people,

it's not enough of a motivation.

Even with drugs or being put "totally under" most people would say "NO!" A million dollars is not enough to make me want to do such a thing! Normally, you and I would want our arm more than money.

What then would motivate you—what would be a white-hot reason—to make you want to amputate your own arm?

Read on . . .

CHAPTER FOUR

How to Know
What You
REALLY Want

We've all heard celebrities and others talk about reinventing their lives. Usually this means they've done some heavy-duty "rethinking" or "redefining" of what they really want.

They've chosen to follow a passion or go in a different direction in their life, in most cases, where their hearts have gone already—or perhaps, to finally fulfill a long-held dream.

Take a few moments to imagine your own ideal life.

- **What would that be?**

- **What does it look like?**

- **How does it feel?**

- **Who's there with you to share it and enjoy it?**

- **Where are you living? How are you living?**

- **How and where do you go on vacation?**

- **How are you going to give to others?**

- **And how are you going to make a real difference in the world?**

All that you just imagined, you can have—exactly as you visualized it, if the following are true:

1. **You want it bad enough you'd do whatever it takes to get it.**

2. **You truly believe you can have it.**

3. **You are willing to follow the steps in this book.**

The Beauty of Being a True Believer

True believers totally believe they can have what they want. They go whole-heartedly after it, too. And in the end, what you and I really believe is all that matters.

How about the person who believes he will fail at whatever he tries? Chances are his life will prove that belief true. On the other hand, a person who truly believes she is the luckiest person in the world and that things always work out for her will probably have an uncanny track record of positive results to prove it.

> **True believers totally believe they can have what they want and they go after it whole-heartedly!**

If you really believe in something, then you are not easily swayed.

If you believe what you want is right for you, then it doesn't matter what anyone says to dissuade you. You press on. **Belief is belief—and it's nearly impossible to argue against.**

What does it look like when you believe strongly enough in what you want that you would literally do anything?

Want to know what it would take to want to cut off your own arm? Here's a true story.

Cutting Off Your Own Arm

Do you remember 27-year-old hiker/climber Aron Ralston? He was all over the news just a few years ago. Do you remember what he did and how he did it? He was the young man who cut off his own arm to save his life.

ABC's Tom Brokaw hiked into the same cavernous, boulder and rock-strewn wilderness, complete with camera crew to have Aron tell the story into the camera and to millions of viewers around the world.

Aron told how a huge boulder had crashed down upon him while climbing in Southern Utah, pinning his arm tightly between the rocks. Aron gave an emotional and dramatic account of how he struggled to free his arm for six days. Having run out of food and water, dehydrated, and fading in and out of consciousness, he made the decision of how to free himself.

His motivation was the ultimate motivation—his very survival.

His life was laid bare and on the line. He wanted to live more than he wanted his arm.

Using a dull knife, he cut through the skin and the nerves. Racked with pain, he feared that he might pass out or bleed to death. He applied a makeshift tourniquet and kept going, being driven to complete the grisly task as quickly as possible.

Photo by: David Rose

Aron Ralston described his self-amputation as a beautiful experience because it gave him his life. What an attitude! What a love for life!

He never lost consciousness and finally was able to break his arm bone by using the leverage of the rest of his body and his own weight. He was finally free.

He staggered and stumbled out of the mountains, walking miles before he was found and taken to a hospital.

Dreams and White-Hot Motivation

Ultimately, we are capable of doing almost anything to get what we want. **Of course, much of the world is influenced by principles, virtues, and standards founded in beliefs—many of those held sacred.** Most of the time, this has a beneficial affect on all of humanity and for each individual living on this planet.

However, true belief has tremendous power and can provide the WHITE-HOT motivation to make you capable of doing even the UNTHINKABLE and the EXTREME.

Suicide Bombers

Here's the simple proof of this.

1. **Do you think that some of the young Al-Qaida followers believe strongly in their cause?**

2. **Do you think they really believe that if they strap on a bomb and blow themselves up along with some infidels, they will go straight to Allah and a paradise to live in, complete with many virgins to accompany them?**

We have seen these acts played out throughout the Middle East and in many other parts of the world.

3. **Is the reward or end result of such an act really the truth?**

4. **Will what they believe as they blow themselves up really happen?**

At a minimum, it's questionable—and logically, it's ridiculous. But the ultimate truth doesn't really matter if you are that young man or women who truly believes it.

Use the "True Believer Mindset" to Your Benefit

■ What do you think would happen if you developed that kind of intense belief (short of blowing people up) in something that would enhance and lift your life, lift the people around us, and make the world a better place?

■ What if you pursued it with the kind of focus that Aron Ralston had to free himself?

I think there would be very few goals that you would not be able to achieve, and achieve very quickly.

I've adopted this "true believer mindset" in my own life. I have had the belief for many years that I am going to live to be very, very old. In fact, I was brash enough many years ago to run a full-page ad in Denver's *Rocky Mountain News*, **with the headline literally promising that I was going to live to be 144!**

Again, at best, that goal of mine is questionable. And at worst, it's ridiculous. Statistics are not on my side. But if I believe it, and it drives me to the point that I take excellent care of myself, then what's wrong with that?

Can you prove that my belief, my goal is wrong? I don't think you can. (I guess I'd better start developing a whole new group of younger friends if I'm going to live to be that old.)

Of course, if I step in front of a bus or die from any cause before the year 2088, you can laugh and say I was crazy and this proves that I was wrong.

Until that happens, you really can't prove me wrong. Again, if my "belief or my so-called ridiculous dream" drives me to do a number of things that enhance my health and my life, and as an added bonus I could possibly influence and inspire others to do the same thing, then I think it is a very good and wonderful thing, for me.

> **Using the "true believer mindset", there would be very few goals that you would not achieve and achieve quickly.**

Do you agree?

Is my "true believer mindset" aiding my health or hurting it?

Believing Something Is True for You

We decide what is true and what works for us. Once you have set up your DREAM LIST (what you REALLY want in life) **don't let someone talk you out of it—because this list, this belief of yours is NOT their truth—it's yours!**

I love the plaque on the wall of tennis champion Tracy Austin, which reads: "The world will step aside for the person who knows where they're going."

Yes, be a True Believer! Believe in what you WANT.

Ultimate Truth for You Is Not Connected to Others' Beliefs

When I was 27, I turned my dream of making a million dollars into a truly solid, focused goal—to make those million dollars by age 30. **It was my true belief that I could do it. I wanted it so much I could taste it. I pursued it every day.**

Yes, many people, even friends and family, said it was impossible to accomplish in such a short amount of time, and by a person so young, and with so little experience.

But you see, all I was pursuing wasn't their truth.

It was mine. So what happened?

Oops, they were right. I didn't make it by age 30! But so what? I knew by age 30, I was headed down the right path. I didn't give up. **I knew, by then, that my belief was to be reality.** I did become a millionaire at age 31, just a year later.

Take Heed of This Warning

Every realistic dream that you don't transform into an actual goal and then pursue leaves you and the world's a bit worse off.

> **Every realistic dream that you don't transform into an actual goal and pursue leaves you and the world a bit worse off.**

Total up the thousands, even millions, of dreams that are unpursued, and you are substantially short-changed —and **YES,** even the whole world. Here's a prime example:

The Saga of Julie Moss

ABC Sports has called it one of the most defining moments in sports. To this day, thousands of Ironman competitors cite it as the reason they want to participate in a triathlon.

It was a few minutes of television that took place in Hawaii, but when it played on *Wide World of Sports*, it captured the world and influenced a whole generation of triathletes.

I was actually in Hawaii at the time, and it was replayed on local television over and over again. **It affected me deeply, inspired me, and motivated me to pursue my life's goals like it was being played out on that few minutes of television.**

What was it? It was the video of a 23-year-old college student, Julie Moss, who was finishing the Hawaii Ironman Triathlon.

She had never done a triathlon before. The Hawaii event is the site of the World Championship of the sport. It is a grueling endurance test. All in one day, it's a 2.4-mile swim, a 112-mile bike ride through windy lava fields, and a hot, humid 26.2-mile marathon.

Julie Moss chose a doozy for her first triathlon. She was doing it as research for her university thesis in the area of her passion—exercise physiology.

A Non-Athlete

Now, here's a fascinating part of Julie's story. She did not consider herself an athlete. In high school and college, she reluctantly participated in sports, especially when there was a crowd. Although she loved the physical part of sports, she dreaded her time on the volleyball court during a game or when it was her turn to serve in tennis. But again, she valued the physical component of the exercise and the good it did her body. She desired to make it her life's pursuit. Thus, her own body became her primary laboratory. She came to Hawaii to see what the Ironman, the ultimate physical challenge, would hold for her.

At the outset of the race, her only expectation—all she wanted to do—her only goal, was to finish. Near the end of the day, however, to her surprise, she was in the lead in the

Julie Moss (see photo) is credited with putting the Ironman Triathlon competition on the sporting landscape with her stunning finish in her first ever Triathlon, Her victory was not a first place finish (she came in second), but was the triumph over self and was more about heart than athletic conditioning or preparation.

women's category. Those few minutes of television history was of Julie Moss desperately trying to get to the finish line.

Literally, only a few hundred yards from the finish line, Julie's legs gave out. She began to stagger, then collapse, get up, stagger some more, and fall again. She refused all help and support from the sympathetic on-lookers.

Just Finishing Is Victory

"It took all my focus just to keep my body working," Julie later said. "The image on television was that I was pretty much out of it. But I was so focused on placing one foot in front of another that I tuned out almost everyone, even the cameras. But my legs kept buckling under me."

With the Ironman finish line just yards away, Julie began to crawl, and unassisted she crossed the line the second place winner. Incredible!

Julie went from non-athlete to a world-class competitor.

Julie's will—her white-hot desire to just finish inspired a

whole generation of triathlon participants.

Thus the adopted moniker among the men and women of the Ironman completions everywhere, is: **"Just Finishing is Victory."**

Her unflinching effort has greatly influenced my life, as well. And it transformed her life, as pursuing something BIG has the power to do.

"That day," Julie reflected in a recent interview,

> **"I learned how much I wanted to finish. That's all it was about, just finishing something. Whatever else happened was icing on the cake. A lot of good things have happened to me because I just got across the line that day."**

Wow! What a powerful life-enhancing statement! We should all memorize it and think about it when we set real tough goals for ourselves. Go back and read Julie's statement once again.

Five Hundred Years from Now

Regardless of your age—young or not so young—your dreams are of paramount importance—more important than you can possibly predict. I don't care who you are or how smart you are.

I just don't think any of us even have an inkling of what impact our carried-out dreams will have 5, 50, 100 or even 500 years from now.

> **Your dreams are of para-mount importance—more important that you can possibly predict!**

If we could look into the future and see the results, I think we would work much harder and longer at sticking with and carrying out our dreams at whatever cost.

Fulfillment

Paul J. Meyer, a best-selling author and master goal setter tells the story of John Goddard who wrote down 127 dreams that he wanted to pursue over the course of his life. John wrote them down when he was only 15 years old.

Some of them were fairly easy. For instance:

- **Earn his Eagle Scout Award,**

- **Type 50 words per minute,**

- **Hold his breath for two and a half minutes under water,**

- **Visit a movie studio.**

Some of them were harder:

- **Milk a rattlesnake,**

- **Read the entire *Encyclopedia Britannica*;**

- **Sail the South Seas in a schooner.**

And many were harder still: climb The Matterhorn; learn French, Spanish, and Arabic; visit every country in the world (he has 30 to go); and visit the moon ("Someday," he says, "if God wills.")

With John Goddard's vivid imagination, backed by heavy doses of organization and discipline, **he has achieved 110 of his 127 dreams so far**. This list continues to "pester" him until he accomplishes them all. How much richer his life is and more fulfilled because he dared to dream.

What's on Your List?

Again, the dream comes first, like John Goddard's list.

You may be tempted to move from your dream phase to setting a specific goal too quickly.

> **Think the dream through to make sure that it is**
> **something you really want, something that you**
> **TRULY BELIEVE YOU WILL DO.**

Don't worry about how realistic or practical your dreams are—or about how exactly you're going to achieve what you want—just:

Dream without deciding—dream without judging.

Now, write it down.

CHAPTER FIVE

Turning Your Dreams into Reality

I t's been said,

"Lucky are those who have passion for life,
but blessed are those who have passion ALL their life."

I don't know about you, but for me one of the primary keys or secrets to keeping young, in nearly every way, is to flood my life with passion. That comes from,

- pursuing what I want out of life,

- really going after my dreams with full force,

- and pursuing my priorities, and doing those things that I love to do with all the energy I can muster.

I set very specific, tough goals for myself and I go after those goals like my life depends on it—because, you know what, I believe it really does. You see, **I loathe the idea of living a life of insignificance—it's like wasting the most precious resource in the entire world—a human life—my life!**

If you don't feel the same way, then ask yourself, **"Why don't I have passion for life?"**

Or **"Why don't I know what I want in life?"**

Those two questions are particularly bothersome if you once had great passion for something you were doing in your life and then you lost it somewhere along the way. Far too many people give up on life.

They fear striking out aggressively in new directions.

They fear risk.

They fear the possibility of failure and losing what they have.

And thus they sit on their hands. They give up on having what they really want and totally miss out on having long-lasting satisfaction, fulfillment, and contentment in their lives.

Don't let this happen to you!

> **Continue to turn what you really want, what you dream of, into specific goals.**

With some new insight and some very directed work, that passion for living can come screaming back and you can keep that love of life and living burning brightly, day after day. **It's all about continuing to turn what you really want, what you dream of, into specific goals and then transforming them step-by-step into reality—your reality!**

First, Do Some Writing

First, ask yourself specific questions, like the ones below. Write down the thoughts that each of these questions stimulate—don't just think about them.

1. Do I want to substantially raise my level of contentment and fulfillment?

2. Do I want to become a better person?

3. Do I want to be known as a person of accomplishment?

4. Do I want to be in great physical and mental shape with ideal health my entire life?

5. Do I want to live a very long, active life?

6. Do I want to make a fortune—a million dollars, or $10 million, or even $100 million? (Think what good you could do with that money.)

7. Do I want more choices and possibilities in my life that making my own fortune could give me?

8. Do I want to leave the world a better place than I found it?

9. Do I want to help others as I help myself?

10. Do I want to travel and experience the entire world and its cultures?

Again write down your honest responses to the self-searching questions above. Develop some of your own "life questions" and answer those.

Unfulfilled?

1. What do you have a true passion for in your life?

2. What part of your life, or past life—even during your child hood—really got you excited, even to the point that you totally lost track of time?

Think about that! **Perhaps you have many unfulfilled passions.** What are they? Do you love music, art, ballet, sports, outdoor adventures, writing, gatherings, or social interactions, running your own small business, or any other super possibility? Now take some time to contemplate and think about it.

Then write down what your unfulfilled passions are. Now ask yourself this . . .

>**"Am I doing that *special something* that I LOVE to do, and am I doing it for my reasons?"**

What are those reasons?

And finally, ponder this:

>**What kind of a BREAKTHROUGH would you be ecstatic to have in your life—in the area of health, wealth, in personal expression, spiritual development—what? And in what would you love to excel?**

Inner Ambitions

What follows are just a few general categories I would like you to run through the gray matter of your brain before we get much more focused.

Look at this list to see what overall categories might jump out at you or might be in the unfulfilled category. Which of these categories are of interest to you and are calling out to you, and why?

Here are some of the choices of broad categories:

1. Artistic

2. Sports

3. Career

4. Education

5. Financial

6. Physical

7. Health

8. Family

9. Social

10. Public Service

11. Of course, feel free to add more categories to this list.

It's not at all unusual for most people to struggle identifying their inner ambitions, especially in midlife and as they get older.

**It can become less clear to you and I
what we really want out of life
as we become bombarded by responsibilities
and daily cares and concerns.
Yes, many young people
have some of these struggles, too!**

However, as kids most of us knew what we wanted or at least thought we knew what we wanted. **But the older we get, the less sure of ourselves we may become**. It is a rare individual who knows exactly what he wanted as a young person and follows that all through his life and never falters, never gets sidetracked, and never gets discouraged.

Most of us, as we hit midlife, start questioning what we really, really want out of life.

Solve Your Own Mystery

To help point you in the right direction and solve this mystery, I have compiled the following questions for you to ask yourself. As you contemplate these questions, be sure to write down the question with your answer.

As you have time, go back and reread the questions and your answers so you can rethink it and let it sift through all the corners of your mind. **Don't get impatient with this.** This is important "inner-self" work you are doing, laying a fertile foundation for that which is to come.

The questions below can apply to virtually any age group or to any person.

1. **What is your natural "bend"—I mean what do you naturally and instinctively like to do?** Forget about any financial constraints or rewards as well as time constraints. **Let your mind be open and flow and just write down the first things that come to your mind.** What do you naturally like to do and are naturally good at? (One of my close friends when asked this question jokingly said, "They don't pay me for what I like to do.")

2. **What did you like to do when you were a kid?** What was your passion then?

3. **What is it that you do now that really gets your juices flowing?** What really makes you feel like you are in the flow? What comes easily to you? Are these your passions? Maybe it's those things that keep revisiting your mind and just won't leave you alone.

4. **What makes time seem to stop for you, or puts you in such a mental state that you lose all sense of time?** What makes you say to yourself, "Please, let this moment linger." Or "I wish this moment and feeling would never leave!"

Take the Time

Now, take the time to dig deep.

1. **Make an appointment with yourself and think through the questions above.** Remember, it takes time—sometimes weeks, even months—to discover what's hidden in the inner regions of your mind and heart. Exactly what is it you most want to do with your life? What do you want to stand for? What do you want to be remembered for or leave to the world? What do you want to accomplish?

2. **Take time to seek advice from others.** Especially from those you think highly of and those who have done some of the things you are considering doing with your life. Go ahead, call those "so-called" gurus—the super successful people who you've always admired, and tell them what you think of them and that you want to spend a few minutes with them. You'll be amazed and gratified at the responses you will receive. Sometimes people who seem far above the masses are more available and approachable than you would ever think or believe. I'll never forget the desire I had when I was young to pick the brain of the founder of McDonald's, who made a billion dollars after the age of 55 years of age. That man was Ray Kroc. I was stunned, shocked, surprised, and pleased when I was told by Mr. Kroc's secretary (after about my fourth or fifth phone call to Padres Stadium in San Diego) that Mr. Kroc had agreed to let me speak to him face to face.

3. **Read and research** all items and areas you can that deal with the wants on your Dream List—the areas that seem to be most relevant to you and your life.

4. **As you read, research, and talk to the right people**—be sure to write down not only what comes from those sources about what may fit your ideal life, but also record on paper or in a computer, all of your own thoughts, ideas, and feelings that come up. This, as you will see, will be helpful and insightful to you later on when you re-read what passed through your mind.

Back to Your Childhood (At Least Some of It)

There are some stunning insights that can be dredged out of our minds from revisiting our childhoods. In our childhoods most of us were pretty much uninhibited—we were so much more spontaneous—we were excited about life as it came at us, and everything was new and exciting to us.

- **We became passionate so easily about so many things.**

- **We wanted to do so many things.**

- **We did not scrutinize endlessly or examine the particulars— we just did it if we liked it.**

- **We became enthralled easily, especially with those things that captured our imagination and enthusiasm.**

That is exactly the mindset that we want to bring back and use in identifying what's really meaningful to us and that causes us to lose track of time when we are truly passionately involved.

As adults, many of us spend way too much time and energy analyzing everything to the point of total confusion. We overanalyze. Talk about a quick way to kill passion.

And as adults, it's so easy to start slipping and do much less with our lives. But at the same time, most of us want to have

> **Whatever your wants are, you must focus and narrow them down.**

more purpose and meaning in our lives, especially as we grow older.

But the good news is as we get older many of us start thinking more about wanting to make a real contribution to the world, one that will last much longer than our lifetime. Sure we want other stuff, too. We may want more money. We may want to be able to influence people. We may want to be able to travel. Maybe we even want to be able to see the entire world at our leisure. There are so many things that could be on a list.

**Peace of mind and deep contentment is a
growing desire of many people as they get older.**

Whatever your wants are you must focus and narrow them down. And while too much analyzing does stunt passion, without any contemplation and analysis we would remain passionate but somewhat flighty, non-focused, and irresponsible children our entire lives.

47

The problem with that is, we wouldn't get much done and we might not even survive—so there has to be a balance.

But Don't Get Too Detailed Yet

At this point, however, don't concern yourself with the details of just how you're going to accomplish your dream or fulfill your passion or even turn those wants into specific goals. That will come later. **For now, just concentrate on the big picture.**

Do you have one big dream or several smaller dreams?

Spend some meaningful time thinking about and defining what they are exactly. In fact, take time right now to do just that even if it takes days or weeks, or longer. **Just do it!**

Creating a list as shown below, recorded in a notebook or some other permanent medium (on paper or computer or wherever), will keep it organized and easily accessible to you. **What you're trying to do is record your OWN BIG picture—your OWN BIG dream or dreams.**

Fill out your List of Dreams side first. You'll eventually move those Dreams that are priorities for you, and the ones that are truly worth your focused energy and efforts, over to the List of Goals. But for now, just list what are your Dreams.

List of Dreams	List of Goals	Your Priorities (a, b, c, etc.)	Deadline (Exact date)
1._____	1._____	1._____	1._____
2._____	2._____	2._____	2._____
3._____	3._____	3._____	3._____
4._____	4._____	4._____	4._____
5._____	5._____	5._____	5._____
6._____	6._____	6._____	6._____

Now, What Is Truly Obtainable?

I'm going to ask you to go back through your List of Dreams you've just made and apply the following test questions to each item. This is a fantastic litmus test to determine what you really, really want.

When your dreams pass this test, they are

ready to be moved over to your List of Goals.

These brilliant questions come from the well-disciplined and experienced mind of Paul J. Meyer. **I've labeled Paul as "The Master Goal-Setter of the United States."** I say that only because it's true, and even now—as he moves into his 80s—he's still going strong, setting and reaching so many goals that sometimes he makes me feel like I'm a real slacker. (Read more about Paul Meyer in Addendum C.)

Are you ready to apply the test questions to your List of Dreams? Here are SIX Questions to ask about each of those items on your list. Write the answers:

1. **Have I crystallized my thinking about this particular item, and do I believe it's truly obtainable?**

2. **Do I or can I have a burning desire—does the thought of accomplishing this item begin to stir a white-hot flame of passion?**

3. **Do I believe I can carry through on this dream?**

4. **Do I or can I have the iron will and determination to follow through regardless of what others may say—no matter who they are and however negative their thinking and comments may be to me?**

5. **Do I or can I have a plan, complete with a written deadline, to accomplish my dream?**

And Paul adds the sixth question, which says it all. Here it is:

6. **Is this prize dream or dreams of mine worth my effort and am I ready to pursue it, NOW?**

If you answered yes to all of the above—then believe me you now have a dream that when turned into a goal will work for you.

"Wait a minute," you may say. "Is this ALL you need for success?"

Okay, there are few other things to consider.

There are some critical steps that will help move you along the path to success, turning each of your dreams and wants into accomplished goals. Each of those will be covered very shortly.

But know this.

**With affirmative answers to the prior questions,
you are already well on your way to getting
from life what you really (I mean REALLY) want.**

The Next Step

So now, if you've spent enough time thinking and writing your Dreams, especially that **BIG DREAM**, and you've tested them against the questions above, and **you've decided which of your dreams are totally worth your**

> **time,**
>
> **attention,**
>
> **and effort**

**NOW, YOU SHOULD BE ABLE TO CLEARLY SEE THE
DIFFERENCE BETWEEN WHAT ARE JUST DREAMS AND
WHAT CAN NOW BE YOUR ACTUAL, SPECIFIC GOALS!**

This is a critically important step and will make a huge difference in both your conscious and subconscious mind.

Now Write Your Goals

Okay, now go ahead and fill in the right side of the list—the "List of Goals." **And here's a key component to writing an effective goal.** If I were writing a goal, for example, to increase my health and this goal would be concerning my weight, I would not just write, "My Goal is to Lose Weight" or even "Lose 25 pounds."

> **Write all your specific goals as affirmative statements with, as much as possible, a measurable outcome.**

Instead I would focus on a specific target like—"I will weigh 170 lbs."

Write all your specific goals as affirmative statements with, as much as possible, a measurable outcome.

After a goal is written down, it is so much easier for you to move to the next step—and that step is to **PRIORITIZE** each goal. Which ones are the very most important to you, and why? Which ones will help you accomplish what you want most?

Prioritize and Assign a Time Frame

Give your goals that priority right now, by placing an A, B, or C, etc., beside each one so you know, without question, which ones are most important to you, "A" being your most important, and so forth.

Then, once you have spent enough time prioritizing your goals, **IT'S TIME TO GIVE THEM A REALISTIC TIMELINE OR DEADLINE.**

This is the KEY to turning a Dream into a Specific Goal.

Using the above weight goal, as an example with a specific deadline attached: I Will Weigh 170 lbs by my birthday, six months from today, on August 15th.

But . . . One More Word About Weight Loss Goals

There's a big problem with weight loss goals. In fact, it's a huge problem—maybe even the biggest problem of all. What is that problem?

The problem is that most people set the wrong goal or at least only half a goal.

Think about this for a minute.

How many people set a goal to lose 10, 20, or 30 pounds and even write it down and set a time limit on it? All the right things so far, right? And BINGO, they actually achieve their goal. Wow—big celebration—tell all your friends—and maybe your case is even highlighted as the testimonial in somebody's ad.

But . . . and this is a really *big but*—because the big butt comes back. **Why? It's simple and may be the biggest single failure of weight loss goals.**

You set a goal to lose "x" number of pounds, and you did it. But that was the end of your goal. If you had set the right goal you wouldn't later join the millions and majority of dieters who gain most, if not all, and sometimes even more, weight back in the following months or years.

Here's the key! If you had set the right goal, or a two-pronged goal, to:

1) **change your eating habits for life to a good, healthy, low-calorie, low-fat diet—and remember the key to the goal is "for life" (a permanent change that is).**

2) **if you had set a goal to get back to your sophomore high school weight, or whatever is your ideal weight, and never, never, never go above that weight for the rest of your life, you would have been setting the correct and complete long term and truly life-changing goal. (Read more about this in Chapter Ten, "An Umbrella Goal for Life.")**

A Bit of Universal Magic

After you've prioritized and assigned a time frame to each goal, the real magic begins. It's at this point, and only at this point (at least from my experience) that certain mighty forces in the Universe and deep inside your mind become activated and are unleashed.

I don't pretend to know why or how it works—I just know that when **I finally move a dream to a specific goal and write it down with time frames attached to it, I am suddenly a changed person on the inside.** It happens precisely at the moment that I truly commit myself to my goal by setting a deadline.

> Once you have prioritized and assigned a time frame to each goal, it as at this point that mighty forces in the Universe are activated and unleashed.

I admire the writings of William Hutchinson Murray, an avid mountain climber, and author of the book *The Scottish Himalayan Expedition*. In the book, he wrote this remarkable statement about commitment and the contribution of these mighty forces in our lives. He speaks to us and all mankind:

> **Until one is committed, there is hesitancy, the chance to draw back, always ineffectiveness. Concerning all acts of initiative and creation, there is one elementary truth the ignorance of**

which kill countless ideas and splendid plans: that the moment one definitely commits oneself, then providence moves, too. A whole stream of events issues from the decision, raising in one's favor all manner of unforeseen incidents, meetings, and material assistance which no man could have dreamed would have come his way.

Murray then quotes this couplet from Johann Goethe's work *Faust* to end his dynamic statement:

> **Whatever you can do or dream you can, begin it.**
> **Boldness has genius, power, and magic in it.**

Begin It Now! The Key to Success—Action

When making your list of your goals, remember, don't worry or think very long or hard about exactly how you're going to achieve the goals. That will come as you move from the goal stage to the action stage.

> **Know this, as I said earlier, there are forces out there in the Universe and deep inside your mind that will be activated to assist you and have the power to fill in the blanks. Be open to them.**

These forces won't be unleashed by just your whimsical dreams or your passing wishes, but only by the goals that you are committed to and focus your attention on—and take action to accomplish.

You might not believe that now, but trust me on this one. It works! William Murray experienced it as he acted on his mountain-climbing goals. I've experienced it too many times to doubt the power that is unleashed within my world

> **These forces will be unleashed by the goals that you are committed to and focus your attention on—and take action to accomplish.**

when I focus in on a specific objective or a move closer to a deadline that brings to life a dream.

More on Achieving My Million-Dollar Goal

At the moment I set a goal when 27 years old to be a millionaire by age 30, I didn't know specifically how I was going to achieve that goal. I just committed myself to achieve it. I had studied a great deal how others had become wealthy, but I was not clear on which path to take.

However, within a very short time I met Larry Rosenberg from Denver, Colorado, who had acquired a tremendous amount of wealth. Larry turned out to be a willing personal mentor, and he was the key to putting me on the path of real estate investing that just four short years later made me a millionaire.

The Bottom Line:

> **Because of the energy surrounding my goal, I believe whole-heartedly that the Universe somehow provided Larry Rosenberg for me to personally meet and learn from. But what made all the difference for me—I immediately took action on what I was shown which led me to achieving my goal, quitting my job, and living my dream.**

The Greatest Book You'll Ever Read

As you go after your own goals,

- **keep notes of not only what you are doing to reach your goals and when,**

- **but also write down your internal dialogue—write down your thoughts, your feelings—YES, even all of your fears, as well as your elation when you have had major successes.**

- **date everything. Make a record of where you are physically as you write. Examples: On flight to Chicago, 3/31/08, or Sitting in my home office, 12:39 p.m. New Year's Eve 2009.**

If you do this, you'll make several discoveries.

- **First, when you reread these writings, you will discover secrets about your own mind and defining insights to some of your internal struggles.**

■ **Next, you'll be able to analyze your own thinking, feelings, and actions.**

And here's the big bonus—the big contribution. **Your own writings will become the greatest book ever written—your book.** And in time, should you choose to share your book with other people (your kids, your grandkids, your friends, etc.), I think you'll be surprised to find that they will think it's a great book, too! And who knows how many people in the world and how many generations will be helped by your thoughts and words?

And if you are normal, you will continue to ask yourself many times over, along the way, **"Is going after this goal really worth my effort?" "Is it worth all my energy and struggle?"**

Of course, that's exactly why you need a "**reasons**" list—or as I call it, a B-RAM™ list (Benefits—Reasons And Motivations) because all of us need constant, frequent, hard pushes from ourselves to keep going. So what will go on your B-RAM™ list? It will be those white-hot motivating, arm breaking, finish-line crossings, benefits, reasons, and motivations. (To work on that one, read Chapter Seven, "B-RAM™—The Surefire Way to Stick with Every Goal.")

> **B-RAM™**
> **Benefits—Reasons**
> **And Motivations**

Unleash Your Inner-Coach

Now, if you've followed each of the steps of the goal-setting formula that are covered in this chapter, it's your turn to experience what's happened to me so many times.

So you've set your goals—and especially that "A" Priority or BIG Goal—and your goals are firmly set in your mind and on paper with time frames attached. Now, you can observe for yourself a bit of brain magic that will begin to take over.

Your inner-coach, that little guy in your head, will not let you forget your overall objectives.

It will...
      remind you,
             push you,
                    and harass you,

until you do what you have committed with yourself to do.

It happens to me all the time. And if I back off just a little, it will "bug me" until I get off my butt and continue toward my objective and do what I committed to do.

Ready to Break It Down?

Now, it's time to start breaking the big picture into lots of snapshots without ever losing sight of the top of the mountain you have pictured for yourself.

So, press forward and you'll see what I mean.

CHAPTER SIX

The Bite-Size Miracle

As long as I live, **I'll never forget how a series of 20-minute goals literally kept a man alive.** Joe Simpson's story is told in his book, *Touching the Void* (and in a movie documentary of the same title), and it is a very gripping, real-life example of the power of goals.

High in the frozen mountains of Peru, with a compound fractured leg (his shin bone shoved up into his kneecap), a determined Joe Simpson crawled, hopped, and dragged himself off a 3,000 foot glacier and over 8 miles of ice, snow, and jagged rocks.

His climbing partner, Simon Yates, thinking Joe had died in a fall off the mountain, was forced to cut the rope to keep from being pulled into a deep crevasse by the weight of Joe's body. Simon then made his way back to base camp and prepared to break camp and go home, sickened by the thought that he had to leave his friend's body in the frozen mountains of Peru.

> **The power of goals can save your life!**

The challenge for Joe was that he did not die in the fall or from the plunge into the crevasse after the rope was cut. Although seriously injured, he began the ordeal of his life!

Without food or water, and delirious with pain and fatigue, he set one 20-minute goal after another in order to achieve his ultimate goal: to get off the mountain alive!

His brutally painful journey off the mountain took days, during which time Joe lost one-third of his body weight and came perilously close to death from pain and dehydration.

Goals That Beat Death

Without those 20-minute goals to keep his mind occupied and keep him motivated, driving him to the next objective, Joe would have died high up there in those frozen mountains.

Joe Simpson would pick a spot maybe a hundred meters ahead, look at his watch and say, "I'm going to reach that spot in 20 minutes."

He would then set off with determination, one excruciatingly painful step at a time, as he kept an eye on his watch. No, he didn't always make it. Sometimes he would pass out and wake up 40 minutes later and be only halfway or less. But often, he did hit the spot within the time limit, which would motivate him to keep going. **Without all of those short-term (measurable) goals, Joe Simpson would, no doubt be dead now.**

Joe Simpson shown here rock climbing, now fully recovered and enjoying life. Photo featured on his Web site: *www.noordinaryJoe.co.uk*

Our Life on the Line

Sometimes I think it's too bad more of us don't have our lives on the line so we learn how to struggle harder and stick with our goals.

But you know what? **Maybe our lives really are on the line.**

> **It's too bad more of us don't have our lives on the line so we learn how to struggle harder and stick with our goals.**

Okay, maybe we're not staring physical death in the face, at least that we're aware of. In today's world, with obesity and all of the physical elements and diseases it causes, maybe that part of our lives really is on the line and we just don't know it.

Perhaps the *quality* of our very lives is on the line. In the second half of our lives, especially, we can easily slow down, get down, stall out, give up, and die too soon. (Like the legendary frog in the water pot that was put on the fire and gradually boiled to death because the water warmed so slowly it made the frog feel so safe.)

A Specific Detailed System

Huge life changing goals can, in fact, create great mental and physical energy and excitement for you—at least in the beginning. But beware, that could soon change, unless you're prepared to take the next step.

> **That initial excitement drives you, but if you don't have a very specific plan to carry you into the future, when you start to run out of that super-excited feeling then you could fizzle—even come to a dead stop.**

The bottom line of all this is that you just can't stop when you feel your excitement waning. (Where would Joe Simpson be if he had stopped?) If you do let the "inevitable drop of excitement" stop or slow you down from affirmative action, then you'll most likely end up being just a daydreamer or wannabe—the kind of a person who only dreams of great things and never follows through to any kind of real

> **Don't let the "inevitable drop of excitement" stop or slow you down from affirmative action!**

achievement. (Remember the frog in that nice, slowly warming water.)

The answer is to create a specific detailed system and put it into place immediately. And you can do that quite easily by breaking your goal down into bite-size pieces.

It Takes More Than Just a Good Start

I mentioned in the last chapter that you shouldn't think too hard about exactly how you're going to achieve your goals. Now, let's become very clear about what that means.

At the outset, when you are setting the goal and as you are coming up with a time frame, **spending too much time** at that point on the details of exactly how to accomplish the goal **may actually deter you** from defining exactly what is the **BIG PICTURE**—defining what you really (I mean REALLY) want and **WHEN** you want it.

Measurable Markers

The key to the specific detailed system you will now create is to break your **Big Picture Goal** down...

**into increments—into steps—into bite-size pieces,
just like Joe Simpson did his overall goal.**

Now, pay special attention to this: Joe Simpson didn't know the exact way to get off the mountain after he crawled up out of the crevasse. Yes, there were plenty of starts and stops, some unplanned detours, some obstacles he had to go around, and some backtracking, and starting over again as he found his way to his GOAL. Those ongoing, incremental, 20-minute goals eventually took him, step-by-step, to triumph.

**With most every goal you will experience
starts and stops and some backtracking.**

Here's the key to keeping yourself going:

- **Set measurable markers for yourself that you know you must reach within a specific timeframe.**

- **Commit to them.**

- **Make them an integral part of your WRITTEN GOAL.**

These measurable markers have the power to keep you on track when the weight of former habits start to pull at you, enticing you back to where you really don't want to be.

**It's the BIG GOAL that gets you excited—but it's
those SMALL STEPS that get you started, keep you
going, and become your motivating force and help
you avoid those deep, "discouragement ditches."**

Remember, these steps are small, and because they are easily measurable, and within a doable time frame, they are very motivating, and keep you moving.

Attracting Resources

My experience is that I receive **all kinds of inspiration and support** from seen and unseen forces **when,**

> **AND ONLY WHEN I am moving—and**
> **when I'm focused and intent on my incremental goals.**

It's as if my action attracts the support and resources that I require to keep me moving.

- **I notice more.**

- **I begin to recognize the resources all around me,**
  and I understand new opportunities when I see them.

- **I seem to be in the right places at the right times to meet the**
  right people.

All those resources and help have been there all the time, but now I perceive them for what they are, because I'm now engaged and moving, not standing on the sidelines.

Daily Tasks

At first, break your goal down into 30-, 60-, or 90-day intervals. **But you're not done yet—you must go to the next step.** You've got to break the goal down into even smaller bites, such as weekly and daily tasks—and yes, some goals can even be broken down to hourly tasks.

> **Daily tasks or daily goals are critical because**
> **they will give you immediate feedback,**
> **and most of us need feedback to keep us motivated.**

The Value of Feedback

If you're like most people, when you're slugging it out and looking for feedback (and this is where the B-RAM™ concept is a lifesaver—see

Chapter Seven) you can easily get tired or bored with the seemingly unimportant or laborious tasks at hand. You may want to quit—or at least slow down.

At that time you might start saying to yourself,

"Hey, this just ain't worth the effort."
or
"Why am I doing this?"
or
"I could be out playing golf,
or
relaxing,
or
hanging out with my friends or family,
or
watching a game on TV."

This is why the feedback that comes from achieving those incremental, measurable markers is so very, very important. That feedback shows you immediately if you are getting closer to your ultimate goal. **If not, change direction, create new increments, new markers that keep you on track.**

Just Make It to the Next Bend in the Road

Ever since I arrived at my sixties, I've been even more sensitive about my health . . . so in addition to my tennis routine, I go biking and hiking.

Last year I set a goal to do 100 miles in one ride. I missed that goal by a few months, but finally reached that goal this last spring—a big goal—but by doing lots of 20-mile rides, then 30- and 40-mile rides, I finally hit my target goal.

But I learned my biggest lesson when I set a goal to reach the top of Big Cottonwood Canyon without stopping. It's a 14.7-mile climb with an average grade of 7.8%.

(If you don't know grades, let me tell you that 7.8% is not an easy climb. In fact, it's damn steep and very difficult!)

Before heading up the canyon, I spent about an hour warming up my legs and body on fairly flat terrain—then up the canyon I headed with my overall "big picture goal" embedded in my brain. I kept concentrating on my final objective. That is, I kept concentrating until I hit the wall at about the six-mile mark.

My legs and lungs were screaming at me, telling me they'd had enough.

**At that point, my head did a funny thing—and
I think the lesson I learned applies to pretty much
all of the difficult goals we put in front of ourselves.**

Surprisingly, my brain stopped thinking about the final goal of making it to the top of the canyon and instead started saying to me, "Just make it to that next bend in the road, then you can quit." But then, when I made it to the next bend, my head said, "Okay, Mark, just make it to that huge tree up there and then you can quit."

> **When my body said it had enough my brain stopped thinking about the final goal and instead set small attainable goals for myself.**

Yes, it was just like Joe Simpson making it down the mountain, except my life wasn't hanging in the balance.

But with all those messages saying, **"Just make it a little further, then you can quit"** . . . I was able to go all the way to the top!

Inner Capacity

I will say, however, that in my mountain biking experience I really was thinking that I would quit when I made it to the bend in the road or to the tree. But somehow when I got there, I just had to go on a little further.

My inner-self was obviously smarter than I was.

Know that sometimes:

■ **Your inner-self will take over and push you toward your goal—**

but also know that your conscious outer-self:

■ **Must start it all off with a rational, big picture goal and then a well thought out plan for breaking it all down.**

Go ahead and analyze what you must do and then start breaking it down into pieces.

What must be done in the first 30 days,

then the next 30 days, then 60 days,

then 90 days, and so forth.

Then figure out what tasks must you finish during the next week to be on track?

Then come the all-important questions:

1. What must you accomplish today?

2. What must you accomplish tomorrow?

3. What must you do in the next hour?

When your goal is broken down to weekly, daily, and if applicable, even by the hour, it's very simple for you to measure your progress. You can grade yourself almost instantly.

Then, you can easily answer these questions:

■ **How am I doing? Am I ahead of schedule or behind?**

■ **If I'm ahead, Yeah Team! A little celebration is due now—a little jolt of renewed determination and, hence, a little more energy.**

■ **If you're behind, Ouch! That hurts. That's discouraging. But that's okay. That's normal (remember Joe Simpson—lots of failure—and some very discouraging backtracking when he went the wrong way—but he had to rededicate himself or his life was over). Maybe you need to try to convince yourself that your real life will be over, too because it may well be.**

Life Is Not a Dress Rehearsal

Remember, this is not a dress rehearsal. This is real life, and it's all yours. And it passes altogether too fast. So make it count for something.

**Make it passionate—make it yours—and
make a difference in the world.**

And remember . . . when you fail, or fall a little bit short, or have to backtrack, that's okay. Rededicate yourself and know that you can do it. Push yourself to get to that interim goal, because, as sure as the sun will rise tomorrow, you will fall short on your daily and weekly goals from time to time (that is if you're human).

That's when it takes even more mental discipline and determination to remotivate and rededicate yourself to get back on track, and if possible, even make up for the shortfall.

> **You will rarely, if ever, reach the big goal without attention to the small bite-sized tasks and goals.**

Do you get my point? Do you see how critical these short-term goals really are?

You will rarely, if ever, reach the big goal without attention to the small bite-sized tasks and goals—all those little steps that add up to you reaching the 29,035 foot summit of your own Mt. Everest. You can do it, but you must approach the task with the right formula for success.

Which means:

1. **Big lifetime dream turned into . . .**

2. **. . . a goal . . .**

3. **. . . which must be quite specific . . .**

4. **. . . with a specific timeline and deadline attached to it . . .**

5. **. . . all written down and spelled out . . .**

6. **. . . this dream turned into a goal will not work without bite-size pieces broken into yearly, monthly, weekly, daily, and possibly even hourly tasks that you can keep track of and celebrate at the end of each period or rededicate yourself when you fall short . . .**

7. ... and for an extra measure of safety and insurance that you will reach your goals, you must use the B-RAM™ concept as outlined in Chapter Seven.

Before we move on to the next chapter, I want to make one final point—and that is, there are so many people who are not really living a full life.

Many are not living fulfilled lives. They're lives are not full of excitement and accomplishment. They are not enhancing or contributing to the lives of everyone around them—nor are they intent on making a difference in this world.

Most people need to take heed of and take heart from the words of the Jimmy Buffet song that says, "I'd rather die while I'm living, than live while I'm dead."

Few people would argue against the necessity and the effectiveness of breaking down all goals into bite-size pieces, because it really does work, but only if you work.

Remember, ACTION is KEY ... and KEEP Moving!

Break it all down into bite-size pieces that make even the huge goals achievable.

Two Simple Examples

Example ONE: How did Arnold Schwarzenegger develop a powerful, muscular body that made him world famous? Can anyone do the same? The truth is almost anyone can develop the same muscled body as Arnold Schwarzenegger.

It's all a matter of following a predetermined set of steps and then repeating them over and over again.

I don't know about you, but his huge muscled body is not my idea of getting in shape. But of course that's not my point. My point is that virtually anyone on this planet earth can do the same thing that Arnold did if he wanted to, if that's the kind of goal he had, if that's the kind of body he wanted. It's simply a matter of weight.

That is, lifting weight. Lifting different amounts of weight in different positions. In other words, adding muscle one ounce at a time by lifting a pound at a time or many pounds at a time. It's all a matter of how many times you are willing to pick up that barbell or dumbbell—and how

> **Set the overall goal first then break it down.**

many repetitions you will do with how many pounds of weight you have added to the barbell or dumbbell—and how long you're willing to stick with the program. **You know the rest. (Set the overall goal first, and then break it down.)**

It is virtually inevitable that you will succeed at building up your body into a massive, muscle machine if you break down that overall goal into bite-size pieces. (Lots of time in the gym and lots of reps with the weights. Certainly, the achievement of that goal would be more assured than for you to win the Governor's race in California.)

Personally, my ideal goal for the physical side of my life is more along the lines of slender, muscular, and very flexible, which is also inevitable and achievable "if I take it and make it" in bite-size pieces. Yes, the routine would be different but the principle would be the same.

A Million Dollar Net Worth

Example TWO: How can you build a million dollar net worth starting with very little—maybe even starting with just a salary.

Can it be done?

How do you break down a million dollars into bite-size pieces?

Okay, let's start breaking up that million dollar net worth goal into yearly and monthly, and even daily pieces. Let me do it two different ways.

The 36/36 Million Dollar Plan

First, let's assume you don't have a nest egg of $36,000, which is what we'll use in this example. But let's assume you have enough salary and/or discipline that you can set aside $33.33 per day. Most people can do this by cutting out expenses—things that they may want, but they can live without—for example: cigarettes, beer, wine, fine dining, or a new car.

Okay, if you can handle saving $33.33 per day, and do this for 36 months, you will have a $36,000 nest egg.

Now I know that may sound boring and take too much time just to get to that beginning nest egg, but don't ever let the million-dollar overall goal slip out of your mindset.

We're just breaking down the million-dollars into bite size pieces so we can eat it.

> **Break down the million-dollars into bite size pieces so you can eat it.**

The next part of the bite-size 36/36 formula is to begin investing that $36,000 into investment vehicles that will return a 36% annual rate.

"**Wait a minute**," you scream! "How in the world can anyone ever hope to receive a 36% return? Isn't that pretty much impossible?"

**Actually, it's not at all impossible and,
in fact,
it's very doable.**

I have not only done it so many times that I couldn't count them—but literally thousands of other people who bought and followed my financial books have done it. (Not only have I written financial books that show you how this can be done, but many others have shared that formula in their own books and show exactly how to make returns of 30% or even up to 100% per year.) See Addendum E in this book for the specific formula, and I think you'll begin to see how it can be done.

Okay, then you might say that if this 36% return formula is true, what's next?

Well, from this point on it's a matter of just doing it. That is sticking with your plan for 11 years, and you're there.

It's a simple matter of compounding $36,000 at 36% for 11 years. See below:

Years at 36%	$ 36,000
1	48,960
2	66,585
3	90,556
4	123,156
5	167,492
6	227,789
7	309,793
8	421,318
9	572,992
10	779,269
11	1,059,805

This chart shows you starting out with earning a 36% return on $36,000, rather than taking three years to save up that amount. This is based on you already having $36,000 in your savings account and you're set to go.

But if you don't—and you don't want to wait three years to get to this starting point—a short cut can be taken one of two ways: **#1 borrow it** from your home-equity or from family or friends or **#2 get a partner** to put up the $36,000.

I used both the borrowing and the partner route to jumpstart my beginning and it worked like a charm. I thought I was really smart and super successful by doing it this way, until I met Dell Loy Hansen, who made my success look like a kindergarten kid investing in bubblegum—take a look at Addendum D in this book, and you'll see exactly what I mean.

So what's the bottom line of all this?

**You must set the big dream and
the big mind-motivating goal,
and always keep the mind-motivating
goal in the back of your head.**

Then, you've got to break it down into bite-size pieces. Make it just 100 meters more, just to the next bend in the road, or make sure you hit your $33.33 set-aside for today.

Now, if you want to know how to keep taking bite-size pieces and never give up, move on to Chapter Seven and learn the magic of using B-RAM™.

CHAPTER SEVEN

The Surefire Way to Stick with Every Goal

Are your goals about doing something wonderful and leaving a memorable legacy to the world or to your family? Starting in your "midlife" or beyond, is it your goal to become a successful singer or actor or a super successful businessperson?

Is it to become a sports star in your age division? (Some rare individuals don't even go to a senior division like Martina Navratilova, who at age 50 along with her partner were still winning open worldwide tennis tournaments in doubles—something that no one in history has ever done in the tennis world).

Is your goal to make many millions of dollars?

> **Did you know that Ray Kroc, the founder**
> **of McDonald's, made more than a**
> **billion dollars after the age of 55?**

Maybe your all-consuming goals center on improving your health. It may be achieving an ideal weight so you can run and move like you did when you were a teenager. **As you know, there are not a lot of things more important than excellent health, and I think you would agree with that.**

There's a Huge Problem

Why don't you do these things then? **It could be that you have a big problem? And most likely the problem is you**.

Yes, YOU—
and most humans on the planet
have the same problem—
themselves.

**People just can't seem to stick with something,
even when it's good for them.**

Many don't muster the discipline and the necessary, consistent behavior and actions to get the job completely done.

Do you start a project or set a specific goal only to give up before you've completed it? Well guess what? You're pretty darn normal.

> **We need to muster the discipline, consistent behavior and actions necessary to get the job completely done.**

Funny thing is that we all start out with such great hopes and enthusiasm and we think we're doing all the right things and we're going to "stick with it" this time.

But many times we don't.

What's missing?

Is there some magic or secret to sticking to every goal you've ever set? As a matter of fact, there is something you can do that is almost magic and works almost all of the time.

What is it?

It's one fairly simple step that you can take that will **dramatically increase** your chances of achieving your **ONE BIG GOAL** (and most of your small goals too), and you'll do it right on your time schedule. What is that step or the secret that will help you make a quantum leap in your ability to see your dreams through to reality? You're about to find out.

How to Stick with All of Your Goals with B-RAM™

First of all,

- **you have to think through what your big dream is and**

- **know for sure that it's what you really want out of life, and**

- **then write it down and turn that dream into a goal with a time frame attached.**

72

■ **after that, you have to add an action plan, breaking the goal into short and medium interim goals and action items.**

If you can say that you've done all of this, then there's just one more step—and this is **BIG**, in fact, it's **HUGE**, and it's the real magic or secret that will enable you to stick with your goal until you've accomplished it.

It's called B-RAM™.

What is a B-RAM™? It's simply this:

It's clearly defining the reasons behind your initial dream—"the why" behind the goal.

If you know and understand your own reasons, and if you fully comprehend that the benefits are worth going after a particular goal, and if you clearly defined and understand your deepest, personal motivations behind the goal, then very few things can stop you from achieving it.

That's what B-RAM™ stands for.
It's your Benefits, Reasons, And Motivations.

You absolutely, positively need to know them and write them down on paper.

This LIST of your: BENEFITS, REASONS, AND MOTIVATIONS is what will push, propel, and persuade you to hit the mat hard, to stick with it, to go the distance.

And one more thing (and I can't stress this enough), it does not matter whether you are 18, 45, 65, or even 80 years old, the B-RAM™ step is critical and will work for you like magic

.

Most experts agree that if the benefits are powerful enough and if we have strong enough reasons, then our motivation will burn white hot inside us to the point that nothing in the world can stop us.

73

So if you truly want to succeed, list the benefits you are going to receive. Then understand your reasons for setting your particular goals. And finally, decide what really motivates and drives you.

Even When You Get Discouraged

In those moments that you may feel discouraged, take out your B-RAM™ lists and read them over. These will remotivate you and again turn on all your mental and physical juices and energy. The likelihood of you remaining down or wanting to quit or slow down will be much less. Believe me—I know it works!

> **Read you B-RAM™ list over and over and it will remotivate you and again turn on all your mental and physical juices and energy.**

If you hesitate or have doubts about how powerful the *benefits*, the *white hot reasons*, and the *ultimate motivations* are to keep you going, then you obviously did not pay close enough attention to the Joe Simpson story. If you missed the lesson in Joe's experience, please go back right now and read again the first three pages of Chapter Six.

Where B-RAM™ Came From

Let me share with you what led to my initial discovery of the effectiveness of the B-RAM™ concept.

Several years ago I was doing some writing and in my research I came across the work of Dr. Roy Walford and his daughter, Lisa Walford. Dr. Roy Walford was the attending physician in the famous experiment of Biosphere One and Two. Dr Walford was also probably the world's leading expert on human longevity. His daughter, Lisa, worked with him. One of Dr. Walford's books, *Beyond the 120-Year Diet*, and Lisa's book, *The Longevity Diet*, grabbed my attention and imagination.

They seemed to be so dead-on accurate about the key to great health and longevity.

I have this wild and optimistic goal and I even bought ad space in a newspaper, so not only would it be in writing, but in print as as well. That goal is that I will live to be 144 years old. Well, finally from the Walfords' books came a program that showed how that was possible.

The basic premise,

> **is that a person who follows a calorie-restricted diet with virtually all foods being of very high nutrient value, could dramatically improve his or her health markers and extend life by decades, living vitally and productively well beyond 100 years old**.

Their hypothesis was proven in over 2,000 animal studies and trials that dramatically expanded the life spans of the test animals. Dr. Walford also showed stunning results in the improvement of the health of the human participants in the Biosphere projects where participants, both men and women lived very well on extremely low calorie but very nutritious diets for several years.

As I studied the Walfords' work,

- **I was very motivated to pattern my eating habits after their research.**

- **However I realized how tough it would be to do exactly what they were prescribing.**

- **It would be a dramatic departure for me from the way I was eating.**

But I also had a goal to live a long, healthy life and I saw their research as a wonderful resource to support me in achieving that dream.

To further convince myself, I began writing down all the various benefits of this "CRON" (Calorie Restricted Optimal Nutrition) Program. After writing down my strong reasons and a number of the powerful benefits and realizing that these benefits had **HUGE** rewards, I was totally stunned at how much more it motivated me to adopt the plan. (Read more about better health in Chapter Ten, "An Umbrella Goal for LIFE.")

In doing this process of writing all this down, I came up with what I now call my B-RAM™ list.

This Is How I Motivate Myself

To me, the B-RAM™ list said it all and as I started running my B-RAM™ list through my mind, it helped me stick to the very sparse diet and kept me completely on track.

**Any time I got discouraged,
got weak,
or got diverted,**

I would look at my B-RAM™ list and it would **remotivate me** and **remind me** why I set my goal to eat this way in the first place.

This has changed my life.

To this day, I have stuck religiously for years to this routine and diet with unbelievable physical results. Not only has my cholesterol and blood pressure dropped and stayed at very low levels, but also my weight is now approaching what it was in high school—down more than 40 pounds from when I started. I feel terrific.

> # The B-RAM™ concept can be attached to any and every goal that a person ever sets.

I'm performing in tennis and other activities like I did when I was in my 20s and 30s. Nearly all my biomarkers are reflective of a much younger man.

To me this was and is much more than a dramatic health breakthrough. It is proof of the dynamic power and phenomenal effects of my B-RAM™ list.

**After that discovery, I very quickly
realized how the B-RAM™ concept
could be attached to any and every
goal that a person ever sets—whether
it's for financial,
family,
philanthropic,
education,
health, or
anything else.**

I have included at the end of this chapter my B-RAM™ list for the CRON diet (CRON stands for Calorie Restriction w/Optimal Nutrition).

I have also included the B-RAM™ list for what periodic fasting can do for a person, based on the excellent book by Dr. Joel Fuhrman entitled, *Fasting And Eating For Health; A Medical Doctor's Program For Conquering Disease.*

As I write this, I'm looking at my Fasting B-RAM™ list as I'm halfway through one of my bi-monthly, two-day fasts. Additionally, I've included my B-RAM list for financial goals.

I customized these B-RAM™ lists for me. So don't worry if they don't fit you exactly.

If you choose to use the great power of a B-RAM™ list, you'll see they will have a maximum effect if you take the time to customize your list so it fits you and your situation more closely.

Three Sample B-RAM™ Lists

As you are looking over the sample B-RAM™ lists below, note that I go over these very frequently to keep me on track. I put copies of all my B-RAM™ lists in several places—my office, my home, even my car.

> **Put your lists anywhere you can easily access them—and I also recommend you insert your list into a clear plastic holder to protect it, because if you're like me, and I think you are, you are in this whole deal for the long term.**

EXAMPLE:

B-RAM™ List for Fasting
Benefits, Reasons, And Motivation

Based on Dr. Joel Fuhrman's Bi-monthly Fasting Program

1. Improved immune system.

2. Produces more HGH (Human Growth Hormone).

3. Extends life expectancy.

4. Creates healthier cells, healthier tissues, and healthier organs.

5. Can actually repair damaged organs.

6. Aides in the healing process.

7. Can slow the growth of tumors.

8. Protects brain cells.

9. Stops the continual work of the digestive tract—so it can heal itself.

10. Lowers blood pressure.

11. Softens blood vessels.

12. Softens and removes cholesterol plaque that lines blood vessels.

13. Fasting has been repeatedly observed to alleviate neuroses, anxiety, and depression.

14. Regular fasting can cure or help chronic neck and back pain.

15. Gives an improved feeling of self-worth, control, and mastery.

EXAMPLE:

B-RAM™ for the CRON Diet
(Calorie Restriction Optional Nutrition)

Based on Dr. Roy Walford's and Lisa Walford's Eating Program

1. Living 150 Years . . . may be possible. At the very least, living much longer and living much younger and healthier.

2. Restore the energy of my youth.

3. No meals for me through a tube when I'm 90 years old or older.

4. No rest home or drugs or life support to keep me going.

5. Most gerontologists agree, with a probability bordering on certainty, that the CRON Diet can extend maximum lifespan.

6. Weight loss is easy if I limit calories to high-quality calories.

7. CRON retards basic rate of aging in humans.

8. CRON postpones the onset of late-life diseases.

   a) Heart disease

   b) Diabetes

   c) Cancer

9. Lowers overall susceptibility to many diseases at any age.

10. I will feel so much better.

11. Won't need as much sleep.

12. Less stress on lower back.

13. Less stress on knees, hips—because of weight loss.

14. Ability to run better and faster.

15. Greater flexibility, i.e. slows loss of collagen and helps joints.

16. Play better tennis.

17. Multiple careers possible.

18. More time with kids, grandkids, and great grandkids.

19. Enjoy my own financial rewards more and longer.

20. More time for financial compounding.

21. Look better.

22. Better eyesight.

23. Feeling of well-being—complex carbs produce serotonin

24. Better hearing.

25. Better sex life.

26. Lower cholesterol.

27. Lower blood pressure.

28. Slows bone loss.

29. Slows loss of dopamine receptors that equates to better motor skills for a longer time.

30. Brain functions at a younger age level.

31. Possibly lowers risk of Alzheimer's and Parkinson's disease.

EXAMPLE:

B-RAM™ List for Financial Goals
Benefits, Reasons, and Motivation

Based on Mark O. Haroldsen's Financial Goals Using Real Estate

1. Prove to self, "I can do it."

2. Freedom from financial stress and worries.

3. Freedom to travel and play when I want to.

4. Freedom to pursue any of my passions or other dreams.

5. More time to spend with loved ones and friends.

6. Obtain a much higher lifestyle.

7. Have a great say and influence in the world through politics and/or education.

8. Enhanced ability to give to others.

9. Help others by providing improved housing.

10. Greater feelings of accomplishment and satisfaction.

11. Opportunity for a new career later in life.

12. Better health and longer life.

CHAPTER EIGHT

Clone Yourself with the Amazing "L" Factor

Show me any super-successful person who has accomplished big things, and I'll show you an accomplished "list maker." **Yes, you can clone yourself by the wise use of list making, plus some good old-fashioned delegation.** Keep reading and I'll show you exactly how.

Of the many specific techniques that have huge value in helping catapult a person to the top, I have to say that "list making" is at or near the top of that list. For some reason most people tend to put

> **Show me any super-successful person who has accomplished big things, and I will show you an accomplished "listmaker."**

a much higher value on just about anything that is on a written list. For example, there's a lot of prestige to being on the AP Top 25 or the *Fortune* 500 Richest People, or the World's Sexiest People as listed in *People Magazine*.

I can't overstate the importance of making and using lists. It's the key to getting so much more out of each precious 24 hours in a day and 168 hours in every week.

It's just flat-out amazing how much more enhanced your life will become and how many more dreams and goals you will be able to achieve, by using lists. And "**daily task lists**" or "**to do lists**" are the key to keeping track of and accomplishing all the bite-size components into which you've broken your Big Picture Goals.

A Pop Star and a Billionaire

I'm sure you've taken note of certain people whose lives seem packed full of many super activities, adventures, and experiences.

Have you ever wondered how they do it all?

Well, the answer lies in
> **making,**
>> **keeping,**
>>> **and working off of lists.**

For example, British billionaire, Sir Richard Branson, credits his list making of the things he wants to accomplish as the key to his getting so much done. He takes the time to go down that list often, adding to it and checking off each item as it is completed.

Today, his Virgin Group of businesses owns about 200 different companies. Among these companies are businesses that specialize in air travel, financial, retail, music, cell phones, Internet, even hotels, and a railroad. That's a lot to keep track of in the business side of his life, but he also has a very active personal life.

> **Lists are one of the secrets used by the rich and famous to support their businesses, and expand their ventures.**

In 1999 Branson attempted and broke world records in hot air balloon travel and in a transatlantic crossing in a small boat.

Pop star Madonna also has a reputation as a big list maker. Although her accomplishments are in different areas than Branson, she attributes her list-making to keeping track of her priorities and getting so much done.

Lists are one of the secrets used by the rich and famous to use every day of their lives, to support their businesses, and to expand their ventures.

List making is a common trait of millions of successful people regardless of race, sex, nationality, or occupation.

**Lists are used to lift their lives and propel them
toward fulfillment—and lists can do the same for you.**

The Critical Path

The critical secret in making lists to improve your life is to do the most important items on your list first.

Yes, you must prioritize.

You must be saying, "Hey, everyone knows that."

And that may be true. But most people simply don't do it, even if they know it! I'm acquainted with many bright and intelligent people who treat virtually everything—every situation, every business deal, and every contact, equally.

They will even let a very low priority phone call or even a walk-in salesperson interrupt a high priority project or meeting that they may be working on. They have no sense of priority. They often move from one small, easy item to another small, easy item (all "C" priority items) on their "to-do" list, just to get them out of the way.

> The critical secret to improve your life is to do the most important items on your list first.

Once in a while, if there is still time in a day, they'll get to a "B" or even an "A" priority item.

Don't Take the Easy Way

Why do they take the easy way first?

Well, they are oblivious to the great power of doing the "A" items first.

But a bigger reason is because the "A" items are usually very challenging—very difficult—and they just don't want to push themselves. They do the easier "B" and "C" items first so they can check them off the list. I guess it makes them feel good or feel like they're getting something done.

**Have I taken the easy road myself to
avoid jumping head-first into those "A" priority items?**

Yes, of course I have.

Only a liar never makes that mistake. Most of us are very human in that department and we slip once in a while. **But by knowing it's the wrong way to approach my lists, and letting my brain dwell on it and acknowledging that fact, I am much more likely not to do it very often.** And when I slip, I am totally aware of that slip and take corrective action. You can do the same because I'm pretty sure you and I are not that different.

I have to say this:

> **We've all heard the old saying about "rearranging deck chairs on the Titanic." It's a lot easier and requires very little thought and effort to arrange deck chairs. Compare that to fashioning some kind of flotation device, diving into the icy waters, and swimming like hell toward the lifeboats that are leaving the scene.**

SO PLEASE, DON'T TAKE THE EASY, NON-PRIORITIZED PATH.

For you, it could ultimately mean the difference between life and death—like the long-term health effects of as ordering in pizza (easy), no exercise (easy), and a movie (easy). Compare that to a stiff workout (hard), ride a bike with a friend 15 miles (not easy), then a dinner of broiled salmon and salad (not as easy or perhaps as tasty as pizza, but if health is your priority, it's a must).

I would be willing to bet you a bunch of money that if you were to study cross-sections of people's lives in the U.S., you would find an incredibly high correlation **between very successful people** and **people who continually and constantly make lists and prioritize them** for most of their life's work and even play.

Not Enough Time?

If you are a person who has said or felt that you just don't have enough time, then you definitely need to read this chapter.

Sure, it's true that there are only 168 hours in a week, and no one gets one second more. But it also happens to be true that by becoming a better list maker—prioritizing every item—and by doing the most important things first—you can get to a point where you could have time "to waste." (Even then you really won't "waste" any time—you'll just spend the extra time on an array of very pleasant, life-enhancing activities—and even have some fun—because you've earned it.)

No Particular Hurry

Just last night I threw a party for all of the many people who took part in helping make my condo development in Hawaii so successful. As the party was winding down, one guy, who is a finish carpenter, saw one of my previous books on a side table and asked, with a bit of astonishment in his voice, "Wow, you write books, too?"

I said, "Yes, I love writing and have written several books."

He continued, "Where do you find the time to do everything?"

He knew I played tennis almost every day, traveled a lot, owned and operated several shopping malls, office buildings, and warehouses, and ran a real estate loan company. Yes, I do all of that . . . and believe me, I'm not any smarter than the next guy. And doing all of that, most of the time I really don't feel pressed for time or in any particular hurry.

A big part of the reason:
I use the power of "lists."

Lists focus my energies and time on those things that fulfilled me and moved me toward my BIG PICTURE.

My center of attention each day is my life's
priorities and goals, broken down into bite-size pieces
and on my "TO DO" list for that day.

You might be saying to me, "Okay, but many people constantly make lists and even prioritize their tasks, and can't seem to do nearly as much as you're talking about."

This obviously leads to the question of what are the other so-called secrets to accomplishment, other than making out a list and prioritizing it.

**The answer is that good old thing
that works miracles called**

"delegation."

Clone Yourself with "Delegation"

If I were to rank all of the different behaviors that have pushed me to the greatest heights of accomplishment in my life, I would have to say that delegation would be way up there.

**Delegating responsibility and tasks to others is a
huge part of my getting more done and accomplishing
my goals. It's often been like cloning myself.**

However, know this. Making lists—as you will soon see—is also a very crucial part of successful, effective, and productive delegation. **There are huge rewards for the person who knows and uses wisely the idea of being "the jack of all trades, and master of none."**

No, not everyone can do this with a perfect balance, and many perfectionist people just have to do everything themselves. But the easiest way to leverage yourself to the max is being that "jack of all trades." But be careful here—you've got to do it right.

Here's my secret to proper and productive delegation.

- **Find or cultivate trusted associates, contractors, employees, service providers, freelancers, suppliers, accomplices, partners, and also many friends and family.**

- **All these people can be the key to making better use of your time and supporting you in moving your goals and dreams ahead at blinding speed.**

Not all of these people listed above, to whom you may delegate, will need or even want to be paid to assist you. There are those who will join with you just because you ask—others would be willing to be involved with you for some extra perk or reward down the road.

**Assuming the person you approach is willing,
and you delegate a task to them, the most important
first step is to get them on the same page with you.**

One of the most effective ways to do that is to make a detailed list of what you want and expect. Also, depending on the person, you may want to share with them your overall goal—let them in on your Big Picture.

Let's Throw a Party

Let me give you an example of why using lists in delegation is so important. Let's say you're very busy with a big important project that is very meaningful, helpful to others, and very profitable to you. The project that you are working on is moving you directly toward a very important goal.

You also know that in order to continue on that path, you'll require more long-term relationships and support from others.

**It is absolutely imperative that you become acquainted
with and create relationships with a variety of bankers,
lawyers, contractors, and financiers—whomever it
may be that works into your future plans.**

You decide that a first-rate social gathering is an efficient way to bring together, in one place and at one time, all those whom you desire to get to know and possibly be part of your future team. This event should also be memorable, first-rate, and complete with excellent entertainment. As the host, this will be the perfect opportunity for you to mingle with each person, get to know them better, and to create a memorable impression of you.

Therefore,

- you delegate this proposed social gathering to someone you trust and you know would do it well.

- Now sit down with this person to explain what you expect them to do. Ideally, beforehand, you've created the following lists—and those lists are completely up to date.

Can you see how simple and easy it would be if you've already compiled the six lists below. Once you've put together such lists, having a big social event is almost an autopilot project for you:

1. **A list of names, addresses, and phone numbers for each of the bankers, lawyers, teachers, friends, associates, existing vendors, etc, whomever you want to invite.**

2. **A list of possible restaurants, homes, and other social or meeting venues.**

3. **A list of the best caterers in town.**

4. **A list of music entertainers and other types of performers or speakers.**

5. **A list of event coordinators.**

6. **A list of all the little extras that you like to have done at a social gathering or party for that perfect touch that you find to be so important.**

    NOTE: With each list that you make, designate your priority choices with the traditional A, B, or C designation so that the person to whom you delegate your "big social event" will know where to go first.

Okay, now the critical part of this delegation formula is to turn these lists over to that someone who is dependable—that someone who has good follow-through—and tell that person:

> **"On the 23rd of next month, I want to invite these people on this list. Here's another list of the possible places we can hold the event, and a list of the caterers, and possible musical talent, and here's even a list of event coordinators if you need one, and a list of the details and extras that I want to have done. You make all the decisions. If you have any questions, be sure to give me a call."**

Also encourage them to make their own lists as they are plowing through your lists—everything from:

- their list of questions,

- to lists of new resources,

- perhaps even lists of more efficient ways to plan or do similar events in the future.

Then you tell them, "And by the way, I do have a 'checklist' that I will be judging your performance by when it's all over and done."

Now this "checklist" is not meant to be a threat. You may even want to make the person aware of it upfront so there is no question about your expectations and desires. And if your expectations are met, if a wonderful event completeley in line with your "checklist" is created, this might be a good time to explain a reward or bonus that can be expected.

> **Let everyone know of the checklist upfront so there is no question about your expectations**

Some to whom you delegate will do it for you without thought of reward, such as a relative or close friend. Some may work for you already

> **But if you do promise something as a reward, do it upfront and then keep your promise. This way you won't burn out a valuable resource or worse—lose a friendship.**

Stepping-stones are great to have, but when they're people, even those you're close to, they will know when they're being used or just simply being "stepped on." By the same token, through your behavior and actions they'll know they're a great asset for you and have gained something for themselves from what they did for you.

Bind them to you with your INTEGRITY and GRATITUDE, along with GENEROUS REWARDS, and they will be more likely to go the distance with you.

List Making—An "A" Priority

So now you may ask,

- **"What is the best way to go about making and keeping lists in the first place?**

- **Paper, PDA, or computer—which should I use?"**

I don't think it matters—whichever one seems to work the best for you. I personally prefer paper. It's so easy to literally cross off tasks or items as I do them. That gives me so much more satisfaction and a bit of semi-instant gratification. For me, paper is a lot better than simply deleting an item from my computer when complete—that doesn't give me as much satisfaction as seeing all those items crossed off, done, and finished.

To Write Is Right and Equals Results

But whatever you use, your lists have to be written down.

That is a must!

You've got to see the lists with your eyes. Therefore, you:

1. Write all your "to do lists" down.

2. Keep adding to those lists as you think of more items.

3. You must continually prioritize your list. I like to use letters for my prioritization (A, B, C, etc.) to denote how important and/or how urgent a particular task is.

4. Check off items on your list as you get them done.

I find it astonishing how many people don't prioritize their lists, or their life, for that matter, and their life's objectives. They treat all items pretty much the same. **Those are not the people who end up being super-successful.** I mean, let's face it—

**there are and should be priorities in your life,
and not all tasks are equally important.**

More Reasons and Benefits

Using prioritized lists additionally benefits you by:

1. Reducing forgetfulness;

2. Making you less likely to procrastinate;

3. Greatly reducing anxiety;

4. Giving more order to your life;

5. Helping you get much more done;

6. Forcing you to work on bite-size pieces one day at a time.

How about one more **BIG** benefit for using a prioritized list. Here it is. It's simple, and yes, you know it already.

Remember,

"To know and not to do, is not yet to know."

Once you have your lists written down, you can easily carry over to the next day or the next week, or whenever, those items that have not been done. **And obviously, most of those undone items better be "C, D, and beyond" on your priority scale.**

**Basically, you don't want to carry over many
or any "A" priorities to the next day because
most of those items should have been done.**

Or at least they should have had some work and progress done on them. In fact, they are important enough that your head should not hit the pillow, until you've earned "checkmarks" by the most important, crucial task of the day.

93

All in One Place

Throughout my business life I've learned that writing down lists in one place is crucial to success (and it should be pretty much the same place). For me, it's a Franklin Day Planner. But any brand will do—such as a Day-Timer or any one of a number of commercial planners available today, it doesn't matter. For you it may be a PDA or Laptop. **But just be consistent where you write and keep your lists.**

I found out the hard way when I used to write different "to do lists" down on various loose pieces of paper (even backs of envelopes or on a sticky note or whatever) that I would always seem to misplace them.

**The amount of time I spent looking for
these misplaced lists was such a waste.**

Master Lists

Immediately transfer any notes made during the course of any day to your master list or lists. In addition to not having to waste time looking for misplaced notes or a list, the master list can now be easily reviewed to make sure you haven't dropped the ball on any particular project or goal.

**I make it a habit to review my master list,
at minimum, monthly—many times I do it weekly.**

I quickly look over each day of my prior week, and in some cases the prior month, to make sure that I've not missed anything. Plus it helps me focus on my overall goals and gives me feedback and is an excellent broad overview of where I'm heading—and keeps me motivated!

A List of Twelve Proven Ways to Boost Your Energy Daily

Now to close out this chapter, the list below is one that pretty much applies to all of us. Whether it's for work or play, family or friend, we all need more energy, especially as we age. So here you go. Here's a list of TWELVE proven ways to boost your energy:

1. Set exciting goals that will put your **BIG dreams into action**— and be sure to add a time frame and an exciting game plan to those goals.

2. A daily "to do" list, looked at or thought about in the morning adds extra energy to your day.

3. Eat more nutritious foods.

4. Drink Green Tea to overcome a mid-morning slump.

5. Get plenty of exposure to natural light.

6. Ease your stress by simplifying your life and mainly or exclusively pursue your life's priority items. Delegate the rest.

7. Heal yourself by being grateful and loving and letting go of all anger.

8. Think positive thoughts to stimulate good neurotransmitters called endorphins.

9. Play and exercise hard to release more endorphins and dopamine.

10. Get more sleep.

11. A few minutes of yoga stretching will give you a morning boost, along with your favorite cup of java or tea.

12. Listening to your favorite music—for some people it may be music with a heart pounding beat—to others, it may be inspirational symphonic music.

I hear this often....

"My goal is to make a Million Dollars by the time I'm 30 or 40 or even 50."

Well, I did accomplish that goal … by age 31. But I had to figure it out as I went along. It would have been so much easier and saved so much time if someone had pointed out to me a proven, step-by-step path to follow.

That's why this page is here

No matter what age you are, the right kind of PROVEN KNOWLEDGE and how to apply it, step-by-step can be THE KEY to achieving a million dollar goal or ANY goal… *and to achieve it in a hurry!*

4 Sure-Fire Steps to Personal Wealth
By Mark O. Haroldsen

CHAPTER NINE

The Key to Personal Satisfaction

Think about this:

- **How would you feel if you played a game of golf tomorrow and shot a perfect score—that is, you shot par on every single hole?**

- **How would the inside of your head handle that experience, especially if it was your very first time playing golf?**

Understandably, you most likely would feel fantastic. How high on the satisfaction scale would that golf score put you? I'd say pretty much at the top! Contentment—oh, yes, you'd be pretty darn content. Satisfaction—absolutely.

But how long would those feelings last? **I'm afraid for most people, not very long.**

Perfect Score—No Fun

Let's fast-forward a week. Let's say you played golf a week later and, again, got that perfect par score. How would you feel then? Pretty darn good, right?

But what if you continued to shoot a perfect par score everyday no matter what golf course you played . . . and you did it day in and day out. How would you feel if it continued and was absolutely routine for you? And how long would your feeling of total contentment and satisfaction last? **I would say not very long.**

Why? Because you didn't have to work for it! That's one of the reasons that almost all lottery winners end up miserable, notwithstanding all the money. They didn't have to work for it—people just don't value or derive much satisfaction from things in their lives that they don't struggle and work very hard for.

> **People don't value or derive much satisfaction from things in their lives that they don't struggle and work very hard for.**

In fact, there have been multiple studies done with the winners and losers of lotteries—and I'm talking big money here. The studies have shown that one, two, or three years later, the losers of the lottery are more satisfied and more content than the winners.

In fact, have you ever read a single story where a winner of a big money lottery has really done anything with their life? Have you ever read a story where those winners, several years later, were full of satisfaction and contentment?

If you're like me, you haven't—not a single time.

The Key to Satisfaction

Lasting satisfaction, contentment, and an increase in passion for life and living comes from taking on tough challenges.

And usually the tougher the challenge the more lasting the satisfaction and contentment you'll receive. **It comes from setting a BIG goal, working hard and long on it, and then achieving that goal!**

You, undoubtedly, know exactly what I'm talking about because you've done it a few times or many times in your life.

The problem is,

as we get older (and unfortunately this is also happening more and more to younger people), we may forget that the *tough challenge or goal* really is the key to keeping you *in the game,* both mentally, as well.

98

You see, if you continue to get that perfect golf score over and over again, it would be so routine that the inside of your mind would not be challenged— you would quickly become bored because it is just downright too easy for you. Of course, the first few times, with all the publicity and the newness of the experience, you would be totally stoked. But that would wear off very quickly.

Several recent studies on the workings of the human mind indicate the brain is stimulated by totally new and unique experiences. It's kind of like that old commercial you may have seen that shows the golfer with the hushed crowd in the background watching him putt the ball toward the hole. The camera follows the ball as it slowly rolls across the huge green, only to show the ball fall into a cup that's about 25- feet in diameter; an absolute dead easy shot. The commercial is meant to be funny, and it is.

But there is a point here:

easy tasks equal low and short-lived satisfaction and contentment.

Difficult challenges (especially extremely difficult challenges) that are met and conquered give you an added measure of contentment, satisfaction, and increased passion that lasts for a very, very long time.

Compare that person who got a perfect score the first time he golfed with a person who worked his "buns off" starting as a kid—practicing endlessly for hours every day and into the night.

Think of the kid who studies the game—takes numerous lessons—struggles through many tournaments with devastating losses and few wins. Then after many years, he or she shoots a 10 under par to win the Masters Tournament. **Wow!** That person's satisfaction and contentment factor would jump off the charts and would likely stay there for a very long time—maybe even a whole lifetime.

> **Difficult challenges that are met and conquered give you an added measure of contentment, satisfaction, and increased passion that lasts for a long time.**

Scaling New Heights

Have you ever met someone who has made it to the 29,035 ft. summit of Mt. Everest? Yes I know, most of us think they're crazy, but maybe they're not as crazy as we think—because their high satisfaction level seems to last for a lifetime!

**Again, the tough challenges and hard work,
over a period of time, equals
long-lasting satisfaction and contentment.**

**One of the big and growing problems
in today's world is that too few people
believe or know this simple principle.**

Or maybe they used to know it and they've forgotten it. Once again, remember the old Zen saying;

"To know and not to do is not yet to know."

Most people, for example, think they want a ton of money—and fast—so they can sit back and relax and really live. They think they want to sit around the pool and drink Mai Tais or watch movies all day. They think that will bring them satisfaction and contentment.

Our very retirement system even promotes that idea. That's one reason we have so many mid-lifers and beyond who are downright miserable and it doesn't seem to matter whether they have a huge net worth or not.

With too much of a slowdown, there's an inevitable letdown, and as you've probably noticed frequently, good old Fred or Mary retire at the age of 65 and die at age 67 or 70.

**The bottom line is,
"if you stop challenging yourself,
you'll start dying."**

It's almost a one-to-one correlation. And all of that starts inside your mind. But if you take the time to "take a trip inside your mind," you'll find there are plenty of ways to program your brain, at least parts of your gray matter, so you'll avoid the trap that snares so many people.

Meet the Blind Man Who Conquered Mt. Everest

Now imagine a blind man who made it all the way to the summit of Mt. Everest. Let me introduce you to Erik Weihenmayer, who accomplished that very feat. He's the only blind man to climb Everest. How high do you think his satisfaction levels are?

But Erik did not just "do" Everest, as amazing as that accomplishment is just by itself. He is one of a handful of human beings, and the only blind man, to scale the world's seven highest peaks on each of the seven continents. Talk about taking on a tough challenge! His so-called disability has completely taken a back seat to his passion to live his life well!

Photo by Didrik Johnck, www.johnckmedia.com

Erik Weihenmayer is shown here at the base of Mount Everest beginning his assent. On May 25, 2001, Weihenmayer became the only blind man in history to reach the summit of Everest. And on September 5, 2002, when he stood on top of Mt. Kosciusko in Australia, Weihenmayer had completed his seven-year quest to climb the Seven Summits—the highest mountains on each of the seven continents, joining only 150 mountaineers who have accomplished that feat. At age 33, he was also one of the youngest.

Erik's award winning film, *Farther Than the Eye Can See*, was ranked in the top 20 adventure films of all time by *Men's Journal*, and brought home first prize at 19 film festivals. It was also nominated for two Emmys. The film beautifully captures the emotion, humor, and drama of Erik's historic ascent on Everest, as well as his team's three other remarkable "firsts"—the first American father/son team to summit Everest, the oldest man to summit (64-year-old Sherman Bull), and the most people from one team to reach the top of Everest in a single day—19!

For Erik and Sherman and those of the team who met the challenge of Everest, head on, and who overcame fear, obstacles, adversity, age, even disability, to succeed, they know that for the rest of their lives they can tackle the "hard" stuff of life and really "do" it— because they've proven to themselves that they can.

As Erik and the rest of the team assembled at Katmandu International Airport, waiting for their flight out of Nepal, sitting amid the expedition's 75 pieces of luggage, they all became very jubilant. This airport lounge became mountaineering's equivalent of the winning team's locker room after the Super Bowl.

With Vision, Summits Are Everywhere

Did Erik Weihenmayer put his feet up after the triumphs and bask in the glow of his accomplishment? Perhaps he did for a few days, enjoying his family. But this former middle schoolteacher and coach never stops challenging himself. There's no "letdown" in Eric.

"There are summits everywhere."
Erik tells many of his audiences he lectures since Everest,
"Just because you lose your sight,
doesn't mean you have to lose your vision."

No Letdown

Three years after he did it the first time, Eric went back to the Himalayas and tackled Everest again, but this time with even a greater vision. This trip he took with him six Tibetan teenagers—a dangerous, difficult journey made all the more remarkable by the fact that these six teenagers were all blind.

Believed by many Tibetans to be possessed by demons, blind children are shunned by their parents, scorned by their villages, and rejected by their society. Sabriye Tenberken, a blind German-born educator and the founder of Braille Without Borders, has rescued many of these children. She established the first school for the blind in Lhasa, the capital city of Tibet. Erik was invited to come and speak to the students after his exploits on Mt. Everest as a way to inspire the students.

He did one better. He invited the students and Sabriye to climb Everest with him, which they did in May 2004. Their adventures are the subject of the documentary *BlindSight*, the winner of prestigious film festivals in the U.S. and the U.K. in 2006.

Let's Take a Trip Inside Your Amazingly Adaptive Mind

The key to continuing to challenge yourself is to continually challenge your thinking. If you work on changing that gray matter enough, I believe you can avoid the slowdown-letdown trap that snares so many people today. You'll be more able to **"go for your dreams."**

> **The key to challenging yourself is to continually challenge your thinking.**

Let's take a trip inside your mind.

**First of all ... do you believe
you can change the way you think
about life?**

**Or are there new ways to think about
your capacities and your potentials and
what you can and can't do?**

Absolutely, you can!

If an extremely athletic blind man can think his way to the top of Mt. Everest, that's truly incredible, right? Of course it is.

But what about the transformation that took place between the ears of six Tibetan teenagers who had been told their whole lives that they were nothing. They climbed Mt. Everest! **Truly, a mind over body miracle!**

> **If six blind Tibetan outcasts can "change" their minds—change the way they think, change the actual pattern and process of how their brain works to enable them to accomplish such a feat—then how about you and me?**

Never forget the work of Professor Richard Davidson and the discoveries he made from putting electrodes on the heads of the Buddhist monks (see Chapter Three) and reading their brainwaves while meditating. Remember, their meditations actually resulted in "the redistribution of gray matter in their brains" compared to those who didn't meditate.

Meditation is fundamentally about quieting your mind—getting rid of outside distractions and increasing your awareness.

As a result of their brain change, these monks were calmer, more focused, and had more control in their lives. Outside influences had little chance of ruffling them. Their laser-like thinking and concentration was a result of a calm inner life and the very way, over time that their gray matter had been reorganized. Their real or outer lives became an actual reality of this and a literal expression of how they thought.

What does this mean for us?

> **Does this study from Dr. Davidson suggest that our minds are flexible and adaptive—that we have power to literally change the course of our lives by changing our brains through a new course of thought—one of our choosing?**

I say, **"YES!"** I absolutely believe that, and I have proved that in my own life.

So now, are you going to prove it in your life?

Meditation and You

Does that mean you should immediately take up meditation? It probably would not hurt.

However, first know this:

> **At its very core, meditation is a very simple practice. You don't have to be a Buddhist to do it. And you don't have to sit squat on the floor and burn incense while listening to Yoga chants.**

Meditation is fundamentally about quieting your mind—getting rid of outside distractions and concerns—and focusing your attention enough that you can have an ever-increasing awareness of your own mind and what it is really thinking and wanting.

Hey, let's try a little bit of that right now and experience what I am saying. Close your eyes and begin to count your breaths, both in and out. Breathe in through your nose and out through your mouth, counting "one" on the inhale, counting up to "four" as you are breathing in, then say in your mind "and" as you exhale. Then start over with "one" on the next inhale—breathe in, breathe out, breathe in, breathe out . . . only thinking about your breathing and nothing else while counting. Do this for five minutes and see how it makes you feel.

As I discussed in Chapter Three, in this kind of meditative, focused, and peaceful state is where I challenge myself to get more of what I want out of life. **It's where I turn dreams into goals with time frames, and visualize achieving them.**

> **The power in knowing what one really wants out of life is possibly the most important thing any human can know.**

Just think of all the implications for you and me and the entire world, if we all followed our own inner direction instead of the hypnosis of society.

Self-Talk

Besides meditation, there are many day-to-day mind and brain enhancers you can use to your advantage. **First, take control of the self-talk or self-chatter.**

Most often, self-talk is negative.

It's hurting you and keeping you from reaching your full potential.

Virtually, what every human being does before doing anything is to run the future action through their mind—sometimes way in advance and sometimes only a fraction of a second before.

Self-talk can either say,

- **"This is something I can do."**

- **"I am so looking forward to this."**

- **"I can do this very well."**

- **"This is going to make me what I want to be and get me where I want to be."**

Or self-talk can say,

- **"I can't do this."**

- **"I'm not good enough."**

- **"I'm not going to be able to pull this off."**

- **"Why do things always happen like this?"**

- **"I'm afraid I will fail."**

As Henry Ford famously said,

> **"If you think you can or if you think you can't, either way, you're right!"**

In golf this is 90% of the game. If you think you will hit the ball into the water, you probably will. **The body follows the mind.** It listens to the self-talk. It believes you. The body says, "Your wish is my command."

> **Your mindset directs or guides a particular part of your life, whether it relates to finances, weight, health, or self-improvement.**

I'll never forget my self-talk as I was playing in a tennis tournament. I got to a crucial point where I knew that I could not afford to double-fault. As I hit the net on my first serve, my self-chatter said, "Wow, I just can't double fault here." Ouch!

What a negative thought! And guess what? That's exactly what I did. I had placed in my mind the thought of double faulting and my second serve went long and I did exactly what I programmed my mind to do. "My wish was my command."

> **The point I'm trying to make is that life is lived mainly inside your head—so you've got to know what's in your mind and how your mind works.**

You need to understand **that you can control** all of the self-talk or self-chatter. You need to know how to direct the self-talk that's hurting you and keeping you from reaching your full potential.

Mindset—Like a Personal Blueprint

A close cousin to self-talk is developing a firm mindset.

That is, before any future event, circumstance, or situation that may come up, because of your goals, you make up your mind about the key decisions you'll make before the future events, circumstances, or situations?

Your "mindset" then directs or guides a particular part of your life, whether it relates to finances, weight, health, self-improvement, or whatever.

A proper mindset acts in your life like a blueprint does for a builder—it directs every decision and action as a house is built, just as a mindset determines every thought that guides every action that, day-by-day, builds a life. A mindset also acts like a rock-hard riverbed, one that is firmly set in place—unchanging—down which flows the river of our conscious thoughts. This mental riverbed ultimately guides each and every personal response to daily circumstances that arise.

Want an example of no or a poor mindset?

Okay, you set a goal to weigh 25 pounds less by your birthday in four months. You're good at following your eating plan for a few weeks. You're ready to fit in those clothes that are just gathering dust in the closet. You have resisted buying bigger sizes for months because soon you will be reclaiming that part of your closet.

But here comes a killer—a bunch of Krispy Kremes—a piece of your favorite aunt's famous apple pie—and/or some Häagen-Dazs Ice Cream is set right down in front of you after a dinner. Oh, oh! You eat it anyway. What you wanted right then took precedence over what you wanted in four months.

What was the problem here?

> **You hadn't set your mind in advance of**
> **what you would do when offered tempting**
> **deserts when they were placed before you.**

The decision must be made, and made:

#1) in advance, and

#2) in stone.

Again, think about the rock riverbed that always directs the water the correct way or a dedicated builder faithfully following a blueprint. **When your mind is firmly set, well in advance, then you won't hesitate for even a moment or try to rationalize any other response other than the one that pushes you closer to your ultimate goal.**

> **If this magic key called a mindset is in**
> **cement in your head, then the likelihood**
> **of your triumph is greatly enhanced.**

The Two-Second Brain Miracle

There's a phenomenal book called *Blink*, written by Malcolm Gladwell, which tells the fascinating story of a $10 million dollar ancient Egyptian find that the J. Paul Getty Museum was looking to purchase. As the museum officials did all of their due diligence to verify the authenticity of this work, there were at least two people who, notwithstanding all of the scientific dating and verification of its authenticity, just didn't feel right about it.

As they described later, almost in the "blink of an eye" when they first saw the work, they knew something didn't fit—they knew something was wrong. The museum went on to purchase the $10 million dollar prize only to find out later that it was a fake.

If you take the time to read Gladwell's book, you will learn what many people instinctively know and practice. (It's even backed up by research that proves it.)

> **The lesson is simply this—what our brains figure out, without us hardly knowing it, can be extremely accurate. Our intuition or our "first impression" aids our minds in figuring out something very complex or difficult, in the blink of an eye—a real two-second miracle.**

Is it a good idea to trust your gut feelings? The answer is . . . it all depends. If you take enough time to set in place what you want your life to be and work hard on your mental blueprint or rock riverbed—your mindset—**then, and only then, you can trust your gut and you'll know in the "blink of an eye" the correct course to take when faced with life's many decisions!**

The Kristin Effect

Another beautiful part of how the brain works is its ability to push you to do things that you programmed it to remind you in advance to do. It's absolutely uncanny how the mind goes to work if you set a goal for yourself with a deadline attached. **I totally believe in the unseen power of deadlines.**

What the brain does at that point you set a deadline is to file the date you've set and then it seems to be able to keep tabs on it.

As sure as the sun comes up every day,
you're subconscious will remind you and push
you to do what you said you'd do by that deadline.

Let me give you an example of that. In fact, this happened to me as I wrote this very chapter.

First, I think you've probably picked up on the fact that I am always setting goals—lots of goals—daily—weekly—yearly—and lifetime. One day in late April, I asked my dependable assistant, Marina, to call the local newspaper and see what the deadline was for me to place a "Memorial Tribute" in the newspaper for my special daughter, Kristin. The anniversary of her sudden passing 20 years earlier on May 2nd, at the tender and sweet age of 16, was soon approaching.

Marina quickly got back to me telling me the deadline was 3 p.m. on May 1st. Well, I kept putting off writing something about Kristin. Still after 20 years, it is very hard and emotional for me think about her tragic and untimely death, let alone write something about her and share what was in my heart. I still miss her so very much. Every time I thought about writing it, a flood of emotion would wash over me, and I procrastinated. But I still had the goal, and the strong desire to meet the deadline, but it had slipped out of my conscious thinking.

> **The brain has the ability to push you to do things you programmed it to remind you in advance to do.**

Now to compound things, around this time frame, I also had set a goal to write a minimum number of pages for this very book that you are now reading.

The date was April 30th, but while I was writing for the book,
suddenly my brain went to work, and out of the blue,
I began thinking about my Kristin.

I started crying, thinking about all the wonderful years I had with her as a young girl and then about the huge "fist in my face" when she so suddenly, without warning, died.

"Wow! Where did that come from?" I thought.

I then began writing the memorial for the newspaper, barely able to see through my tears. I wrote furiously without stopping and within a few minutes I was done. My goal had been fulfilled right on time.

Mark's Newspaper Memorial for Kristin

Kristin Haroldsen
September 30, 1969–May 2, 1986

To all those reading this, I know this much about you— You know how precious life is, and you understand that your fond memories of the loved ones in your life who have passed on are so very sweet for the time you had with them, but somewhat bitter for the years without them. Sometimes even now, 20 years later, it hurts so very deeply. But we all learn to live with the absence of our "dearly beloved" one.

Kristin, I miss you. I love you so very much, as do all who knew you. You blessed our lives and made them so much richer for having known you, for those 16 years that passed in a flash. Maybe we will see you again. With the greatest of love—your daddy, Mark O. Haroldsen—your mommy, Lois Ann Haroldsen—your brothers, Mark E., David O., Marcus, and George—and your sisters, Nichol, Camille, and Lindsey.

Here's the interesting part of all this. In my enthusiasm to work on this book, I had virtually forgotten about my deadline for Kristin's memorial tribute.

But there it was before me, all finished, and written from the heart.
My words were exactly what I really wanted to say, too.

The Brain Works Non-Stop

I'm totally convinced that my brain had been working without a break to fashion the words to be said, and supplied them just at the right moment that they were due.

I am totally convinced that your brain, and everyone's brain, works just like that, too.

Magically, right after finishing the tribute for Kristin, I moved to the kitchen counter and began writing about this whole experience that fits in perfectly with this very chapter about your "amazingly adaptive mind." I do believe we're all pretty much the same and our brains work much like everyone else's. It's down right scary and great all at the same time. What's the basic lesson here? **Trust your mind!**

It will be working, non-stop, subconsciously, on even those things that seem to come to you in the "blink of an eye."

Choosing Our "Mind Roads"

We can choose not only the words of the self-talk we run through our minds, and the thoughts that those words create, but we have the great power to choose an entire series of thoughts or what I call a "mind road."

Our brains remember things by
linking thoughts or words together.

If you find your mind wondering down a road that you've traveled before that leads you to sorrow or sadness or is very harmful in any way for any number of reasons, **you can consciously choose to stop right there,** and say to yourself, "No, I don't want to go down that road."
You can quickly back up and start down another road, mentally.

112

I will never forget when I was in Kansas City giving a speech, shortly after the death of Kristin. It was near Christmastime and after the speech I was alone in my hotel room, finding myself "going down a road" that I had gone down a thousand times before. I started thinking about Kristin, missing her so desperately. I knew where this thinking was going, as it had gone so many times before, leading to an emotional breakdown or minimally a huge visitation of sadness and sorrow.

That evening, however,
I discovered the great power of stopping that cycle.

I suddenly realized what I was doing to myself and knew I had a choice. I immediately stopped—backed up and chose another mental road to drive down. The road I chose that particular night, and have used many times since, was a tennis road. Mentally, I started playing tennis in my mind and practicing my backhand, forehand, and serve. I visualized playing a whole match in my mind. Yes, and I chose to win the match.

This pulled me out of my negative and depressive, emotional spiral.

I love Kristin so much. But she is gone.

> **We have the power to choose an entire series of thoughts or what I call a "mind road."**

No amount of grief on my part will bring her back. It won't change the fact that she is not with me. But I am alive—and I believe she would want me to live and enjoy life, as she did. I love tennis and feel so alive when playing it. As a mind road, it was perfect. **It is a lifesaver to me whenever I begin to be overcome by grief or sorrow or regret.**

If used correctly, choosing "mind roads" that are very positive can be a real benefit to you in everything you do.

Greater Satisfaction

Regardless of what your overall self-talk, mindset, or mind roads have been up until now, **I want you to take time to rethink that overall structure.**

Why?

Because it's so easy to let that blueprint change over the years. How does it change? In many, if not most cases, we begin to lower our "challenge levels." Yes, don't allow your mind to accept the premise that it's okay to challenge yourself less and less. **Don't look for the "easy path."**

You see as you consciously accept the easier path, your inner-brain begins to change your inner-blueprint and subtly changes the course of your mental riverbed—and depletes your level of commitment. When that happens, you gradually begin to lose a degree of enthusiasm and passion for almost anything you do.

> **Losing some passion for living has a**
> **direct correlation to the amount of**
> **challenge you are taking out of your daily life.**

A huge part of your life and my life is lived inside our craniums. So it just makes common sense to always be aware of what's going on in there so we can readjust our inner-blueprint or mindset when it slips off the course that brings us anything less than maximum satisfaction, long-term contentment, and passion for living.

There's much more at work, much more going on behind the scenes than you realize or give your brain credit for.

- **Firmly set your mind.**

- **Create the self-talk that pushes you ahead.**

- **Commit to a mental blueprint or mindset that is formed accurately and precisely to fit your dreams, ambitions, and your goals.**

YOUR MIND MUST MIRROR WHAT YOU REALLY WANT YOUR LIFE TO LOOK LIKE AND BECOME.

CHAPTER TEN

An Umbrella
Goal for LIFE

Here's an umbrella goal for your life and my life. And believe me this goal supports all other goals. In fact, you and I will most likely die without it—or at least die much younger than we should. At a minimum, without this goal, we may live quite miserably as we get older.

This goal is that serious—that important!

What I'm about to tell you, we've all heard a thousand times. We know it's a basic truth. A growing number of people (especially in the United States) are further away from achieving this goal than ever before.

What is this so-called umbrella goal, the goal that makes virtually everything else in your life work—and work well?

I'll get to that answer in a minute—but first let me tease you a bit more.

You can see the results everywhere of those who don't set and achieve this goal—from rich people to poor people. In fact, you see people who have set lofty and very worthwhile goals, even achieve them or are on the brink of great personal success, and then bang, they die or their health goes to pot and they can't really enjoy any of their success or even enjoy life at all.

What I'm talking about is your health—physical and mental.

This is the great **UMBRELLA GOAL FOR LIFE**—your life:

- **To have good health all your life,**

- **To live to a ripe old age with vigor and passion, sucking out every precious moment that life has to offer,**

- **And living life to its fullest is what your after!**

You know the old saying:

"Without your health, you have nothing."

That statement, of course, isn't totally true. There are a lot of those incredible people who do amazing things and live amazing lives while in poor health. But for the vast majority of people, great health is absolutely critical to a satisfying and enjoyable life.

I'm not saying that you can control all things when it comes to your health and how long you're going to live, but you can control more than you may think. That's what this chapter is all about.

Sickness Sucks Your Sparkle

You may know from your own personal experience that when you're really sick or down or depressed, life loses almost all its sparkle. You lose all your passion for living. Nothing sounds fun or exciting. All you care about is being well.

Yet look at what so many of us are doing to ourselves that's devastating to our health—and as a natural consequence, our passion for life is killed by our choices along the way. What is it that we're doing? I'll tell you in one simple sentence.

We are "digging our own graves with our forks and spoons."

Of course, part of the reason we're digging our own graves is because we view so much negative motivation from TV ads, and to top it all off we're becoming a nation of almost totally inactive, sedentary people who are in danger of losing the use of our legs and maybe even our arms.

Does this sound extreme?

Not if you look at the health statistics as people age today.

**What we put into our mouths is directly related to the
horrendous increase in cancer, diabetes, heart
disease, and so many other debilitating diseases.**

"Yeah, but," you may counter, "life expectancy is also on the rise." Yes, that's true, at least for the moment—but only as long as prescription drugs continue to be pumped into us and we continue to build "long-term care" facilities in record numbers.

But something else is happening right now!

**Did you know that life expectancy
is projected to begin shortening
with the generation that is now being born?**

I'm also talking about the "quality" of life that you and I will be living as we get older. It doesn't make much sense, to pursue wonderful objectives and reach for and achieve lofty goals just to end up in the cardiac ward at age 48, or 55, or even 67. It's equally a waste to suffer endlessly from arthritis, Type 2 diabetes at young ages, or to get cancer at any age—especially if these things can be avoided.

Wouldn't you agree?

Personally, I absolutely refuse to fall apart physically or mentally and I do have some choice in those kinds of matters. Furthermore, I refuse to die until I'm totally finished living the healthy, wealthy, and contented way I choose to live.

Hard to Get Out of Your Rolls Royce?

I've seen people who have made $5million dollars by the age of 45, but they are so overweight and out of shape that they can hardly get out of their Rolls Royce, let alone run and play with their kids. How sad it is to live in a nation with such great freedom, great opportunities, and great technology, and yet not be able to enjoy it to the fullest because so many are suffering physically or mentally.

Someone once said,

"Life is too short to live little."

But I say,

"Life is too short to be unhealthy for even a day!"

It doesn't have to be that way. **And I suppose the good (and bad) news is that only you can change the outcome.** Whether you're dirt-poor or have $5 million dollars or even a billion dollars, no one can improve your health for you.

You absolutely have to choose your own good health and ... create it for yourself.

If rich people could hire someone to go to the gym and work out for them or they could magically transfer all the extra calories from fattening foods they enjoy to someone else, there definitely would not be any fat millionaires or multi-millionaires.

I'm sure many of these millionaires are totally surprised or even shocked when they realize that even with all their money, absolutely no one—and I mean no one—has a free pass or an easy way to great health and longevity without putting forth their own individual effort.

> **No one has a free pass or an easy way to great health and longevity without putting forth effort.**

Here, at last, is a part of life that places everyone pretty much on a totally level playing field. I like that.

Every human, regardless of his or her I.Q., wealth, education or family connections has to work this one out on his or her own. Who you know will not help you very much when it comes to your own health.

However, those people you hang out with can have a huge influence on you and your health (yes, we tend to follow the habits of "the group" or "our associates")— so pick your friends and associates carefully.

Mindset Sets Habits

For example, I made it a point, after reading *The Longevity Diet* by Lisa Walford, to get to know and spend time with Lisa.

**Yes, I wanted some of her knowledge, influence,
and habits to rub off on me—and guess what?**

They did.

Her book is not only a great read, but more importantly, its conclusions on extending a person's maximum lifespan by an amazing percentage is based on over 2,000 animal studies that tested various diets in laboratories around the world. And as you might expect, great health and a maximum lifespan is the natural outcome of this longevity diet.

> **Great health and a maximum lifespan is a natural outcome of the "Longevity Diet."**

But to achieve both super-health and a maximum lifespan, you must set a specific goal for that—**and yes, you must write it down and fashion an action plan to turn the goal into your own healthy reality.** (If you really want to pursue this to a degree that 99% of earth's population doesn't even consider, you may want to read Ray Kurzwell's book entitled *Fantastic Voyage: Live Long Enough to Live Forever.*)

Probably the three biggest reasons most people can't seem to stick with a healthy diet are:

1. They really don't commit to their new eating and health goals and cement them solidly in their minds.

2. They don't record their plan, let alone frequently review it and all the Benefits, Reasons, and Motivations (B-RAM™) for sticking with their nutrition and health goals.

3. This is a big one! They see their new diet as a "temporary thing." You know what I'm saying? Many think, "Well, as soon as I get down to the weight I want to be, then I can go back to eating all that tasty food I've been missing out on." Huge brain mistake! The word "diet" for most of us has come to mean something short-term. A hundred years ago a diet meant a person's permanent eating habits, and that's how you need to look at it today if you're going to be successful.

HINT: Look at your everyday diet through the eyes of long-term health, NOT, "I just want to lose weight." Think primarily of your health and longevity, hence you will be much more likely to stick with it long after you've reached your ideal weight. And believe me, with a truly healthy diet you will lose weight, especially with the near perfect longevity diet.

I invite you to look at changing your diet today, and create it as part of an umbrella goal for your life—that is if you plan on being successful in all the other areas of your life and enjoy some longevity here on this planet.

Now, let's move on.

"What else besides diet," you may ask,
"is included in this all-important umbrella goal
that will keep me alive and passionate and healthy?"

Movement Is a Must

For most of us, if we're able to move around with ease, we feel so much more alive—which makes us feel very independent and in control of our lives.

When we're up and moving it's so much
easier to be passionate about life and living.

But

When we are sedentary, sick, or stuck in one place,
it usually brings us down.
This can be the gateway to the depths of depression

.

I can certainly feel for the paraplegic or the quadriplegic and admire those who battle through paralysis and grab hold of life, anyway they can, actively creating a place for themselves in the world. In many cases, their trials actually strengthen them, pushing them toward accomplishment and excellence.

All of these incredible people deserve our admiration and an Olympic Gold Medal.

I also see the blind, the deaf, and those who may have struggled from birth, taking charge of their lives. They literally keep moving, regardless of their disability, like Erick Weihenmayer (see Chapter Nine) and his blind ascent of Mt. Everest. They inspire us.

But for most of us who are capable of walking, seeing, and using our capacities there is a huge correlation between bodily motion and our mental and physical well being.

My Hip Story—The Perfect Example of How to Quickly Feel Old

Pretty much everything in my life was in a near-perfect flow—family, finances, friends, and fun. But then I began to notice stiffness in my right hip. Over the months, that stiffness grew into a low-grade pain. My range of motion became so limited that I couldn't even cross my legs and getting in and out of a car became more and more difficult.

"This is ridiculous," I thought. "I've just got to workout more and add stretching and yoga to my routine." I not only did exactly that, but I also began consuming more and more ibuprofen. Big disappointment—it didn't work!

Over the next 12 months, the pain and stiffening not only got worse, but my left hip was getting almost as bad as my right one.

It got so bad that I couldn't get out of a chair without using my arms or getting a helping hand from someone else. I even had to crawl out of my car more than a few times when my hip totally locked up on me. WOW, that was painful!

> **My physical condition was not the real problem. The real problem was what it was doing to the inside of my head.**

But what really pushed me to doing something about it, was what my oldest son, Mark Ed, said to me one day. "Dad, you don't walk ... you waddle."

Ouch! That hurt. But his comment was the catalyst for me to take a lifesaving action for myself—hip surgery.

But please don't miss the main point here. It's not just about my arthritic hips. It's more about what my arthritic hips were doing to the inside of my head.

You see, I was at the point where my lack of ability to move made me believe I was very old. And I had become old very quickly.

■ It affected my thinking.

■ It changed my life.

■ It pushed me into a pit of depression. It started as something external, but it turned into an inside job, inside my brain.

Massacring Movement

Now, if this physical condition had happened only to me, I may not even be writing about it. But it's also happening to many millions of people. No, I don't mean just bad hips or bad knees or terribly painful low back pain (although those are problems for many people), but there's an even bigger problem—a huge and growing problem—it's the insidious, sneaky thing that's hitting millions and millions of people, and the cause of many of distressing maladies, today.

I'm talking about being "overweight" or worse "obesity."

If you are just a little overweight and still moving around just fine and thinking "all is well," listen to this:

YOU ARE NOT AS WELL OFF AS YOU MAY THINK.

So sorry!

Get a load of this:

in 2006, a 10-year study of 500,000 members of the AARP found that Americans at age 50, who "carry even a few extra pounds" raise their risk of dying early by 20–40% more compared to those who are at their optimal weight.

Of course we've known for a long time that obese people are more likely to develop heart disease, cancer, and diabetes, but this new study shows that even a few extra pounds can be a killer too.

This gigantic, growing problem can also begin to severely minimize your movement. Eventually, it will even massacre it—and as your movement begins to be minimized, (if you're like me) you begin to think of yourself as **"prematurely old"** and getting older at a rate that is down right scary.

Once again, I say, it doesn't have to be that way.

Just before I went into surgery to have both of my hips replaced, my surgeon, Dr. Harland Amstutz, said,

> **"Now Mark, let me give you some critical advice—the most important thing you can do after you recover from surgery is to keep the weight off."**

Now understand, I wasn't obese—at six feet tall I weighed then between 192 and 195 pounds. I was a bit heavy, but I was in pretty good shape. My ability to move better without putting excess strain and stress on my new hips was directly related to my body weight. This, of course, is true for all of your weight-bearing joints, whether you've had surgery or not.

That decision to correct my arthritic hips, along with my permanent change in my diet, and continued workout activity, has changed my life more than I could ever explain on paper.

- **It's much more than looking better now at between 165 and 170 pounds.**

- **It's more than feeling great from my healthier diet.**

- **And it's even more than my pain-free movement, and in creased flexibility, range of motion and energy.**

- **It's much more than all of that!**

What is it? It's that good old inside job that's affecting the inside of my head.

Being able to move took years and years off my age. Yes, physically—but even more so mentally. I feel young again, very young! It was suddenly like I was a kid again. I could run and jump and play.

WOW, what a feeling! And believe me, at almost 65 years old, the ability to move so easily and freely is so much more appreciated than when I was a kid. Didn't we all take that "ease of movement" for granted back then?

Slowly losing the ability to move from bad hips is no different than a person who slowly and subtlety losing their ability to move because of gaining extra pounds.

But the good news is that it doesn't have to stay that way.

And remember, without setting this kind of goal (a goal for phenomenal health) and sticking with it, you'll die too early or be severely limited, as you get older.

**Great and abundant health really
is an Umbrella Goal For Life.**

Okay, now if you agree with me, and you want to do something about it, let me give you a few of the life-saving tips and directions that I have learned from personal experience and have gathered from some very smart people.

Slow the Aging Process

The Only Proven Way To Slow The Aging Process And Maintain Vitality is the subtitle of Lisa Walford and Brian M. Delaney's book *The Longevity Diet*. And you know what? This is a claim that is backed up with some great research. My first strong recommendation is that you go out and get their book and read it carefully.

> **Great mental and physical health has to be earned the hard way, one step at a time, with very consistent effort**

In the meantime, let me give you as much insight as I possibly can into what you need to do about this life-enhancing, life-extending, and vitality-building umbrella goal.

124

Most people know that good health is all about diet and exercise. But too many people get lost in the details. They want to believe that there is a magic pill or a new fad diet that is going to solve their problem quickly and without much effort on their part.

Instinctively, I think you and I know that's not ever going to happen. That kind of childish, wishful thinking reminds me of the people who are always looking for that one big financial homerun that will bring them millions of dollars overnight!

HEY, IT JUST AIN'T GONNA HAPPEN.

Likewise, great mental and physical health has to be earned the hard way, one step at a time, with very consistent effort.

Boosting Dopamine and Serotonin

Sure, there are some so-called secrets that make it a little easier. For example, here's a little depression-beating health secret.

1. **As a person ages, there is a tendency for the body to produce less and less dopamine and serotonin, and of course these are critical chemicals in the brain that make you feel good.**

2. **When we have less and less production of dopamine and serotonin in our body, it makes it harder for the brain to process thoughts in an accurate and positive manner.**

3. **Consequently, as people age they tend to get down and depressed more easily. Because of the shortage of dopamine and serotonin, their brains can take a neutral or positive event, situation, or thought and twist it into only seeing the negative side.**

Secret One

There is a simple and healthy solution to this growing problem? According to Susan Algert, PhD, an assistant professor of the Human Nutrition & Food Science Department at California State Polytechnic University, **the answer lies in what you eat.** My own personal experience bears this out.

■ For example, eating lean protein in the morning will boost your levels of dopamine and raise your energy at the same time.

■ Eating complex carbohydrates in the afternoon raises your serotonin levels.

■ Consequently, I have adapted my own personal habits to reflect that knowledge and those facts.

1. Almost every morning I make one or more meat and cheese wraps, using three thin slices of no-fat turkey (40 calories), wrapped around a low-fat *Laughing Cow* cheese (35 calories), for a total of 75 calories per wrap, or seven to nine pieces of delicious shrimp which is low-calorie and high-protein. This not only mentally raises me up; it also doesn't add a lot of calories to my diet. At the same time it does not raise my blood sugar so I feel satiated.

2. Then, every afternoon, I fix a fruit and veggie shake or eat a small serving of whole-wheat pasta with some fruit and vegetables on the side.

Secret Two

For secret number two, I'm going to push you again to read *The Longevity Diet*. Is it for everybody? Absolutely not. Why? Because many people don't think that near-perfect health is worth the great effort required to put into it. And, hey—as the Hindu philosophy will tell you, "that's okay" if that's where a person is focused at the moment. Let them be with that. And if they think they can't, they're right!

But what about you?
Are you one of the few who think you can?

Of Mice and Men

It would be really easy to do what Lisa Walford and Brian Delaney say in *The Longevity Diet*, if you were a rat or a mouse or a monkey. These animals are precisely the ones that have been used to provide undeniable scientific results in one of the biggest health and longevity studies on planet Earth.

If you knew that by following the same diet that those animals were restricted to, you could add an extra 25 to 40 healthy years to your life, do you think you could or would change your eating habits?

**The mice didn't have a choice—but you
and I do—which, of course, makes it all the harder.**

That's the big life or death question, isn't it? It's a bit of a surprise (at least it was for me) that most people won't make that change. Why? Well—because it's not easy.

42 Days to Totally Change Your Life

What is so hard about it? Well, the key to the longevity diet is something that doesn't sound very good, but is so very, very good for you.

It's called "calorie restriction."

OUCH!

Lot's of people, in fact most people, just like their food way too much and wouldn't entertain the thought of calorie restriction.

But guess what? Once you really change your "habits" it gets a lot easier. And maybe it's a bit comforting for you to know that it only takes about six weeks to firmly form a new eating habit. Don't forget about good old professor Richard Davidson (Chapter Three) and his discovery of how one can permanently change the brain.

> **It only takes six weeks to firmly form a new eating habit. Once you change your habits it get a lot easier.**

**Therefore, if you can stick with it for six weeks,
or 42 days, you can totally change your life.**

And oh, by the way, the calories that you do eat absolutely must be jam-packed with maximum nutrition, because a severely "nutrient restricted" diet will shorten life rather than lengthen it. For those of you who will follow this regimen, there are no more or very few "empty calories."

This has been a very, very brief summary of *The Longevity Diet* for you. Now go, get the book and read every line—and see for yourself the proof of many more healthy years for you. Also with eating this diet comes a huge decrease in your odds of getting cancer, heart disease, or just about any other disease.

Decide how many healthy years you want to add to your life, and then begin the diet for the rest of your life by choosing the level that fits you best—also choose the level of calorie restriction that you can stick with.

Exercise vs. Calorie Restriction

Okay, how about the exercise part? How important is it? Well, first of all this may surprise you, as it did me:

If you had to choose calorie restriction versus a lot of exercise to attain a longer and healthier life, animal studies prove beyond doubt that eating less calories (but calories that are very nutrient packed) will lengthen your life and cut disease by a huge factor compared to exercise alone.

Now that doesn't mean that exercising is bad or won't improve your health—but if you think you can gorge yourself and exercise it off, you're just flat-out wrong as far as health and longevity are concerned.

Oh, to be a rat or a monkey and not have to think about all this . . . or have to make decisions! You'd think that we humans could change our habits a bit without being forced to do so like the rats and the monkeys. Sometimes, in my wild moments, I think of a few people I know who could use a little monkey cage to improve their lives by forcing some habit changes.

So, yes, add exercise (and stretching) to your routine but keep it in moderation—and as everyone knows, exercise will boost your endorphin levels so you get extra mental benefits from even moderate amounts of exercise.

Let me finish this chapter with a summary list of health and longevity hints that have been extremely helpful to me. These notes and ideas are from Joel Fuhrman's book *Eat To Live*, from Lisa Walford's book *The Longevity Diet*, and from my own experience:

1. Try to keep your daily calorie intake to 30–40% less than average (for me, that's 1500 to 1750 calories per day).

2. Know that your body, over time, will adjust to fewer calories.

3. Raw vegetables are the biggest anti-cancer foods that exist.

4. Make a written contract with yourself as to your health and eating habits and review it monthly.

5. No more than 10% of your diet should come from animal products.

6. Meat, poultry, dairy, and eggs are all linked to arthritis, depression, and other diseases.

7. Studies show that as fruit and veggie consumption increases, chronic diseases and pre-mature death decreases.

8. A poor diet can be connected to depression, and many times is. A highly nutritious diet can help overcome depression.

9. Make a point to eat foods that help boost dopamine and serotonin:

Dopamine Boosters	Serotonin Boosters
Fish	Whole Grains
Turkey*	(whole wheat and brown rice only)
Eggs*	Fresh Vegetables (especially root
Beans and Legumes	crops and squash)
Soy	Apples and other fresh fruit
Coffee	Bananas
Green Tea	Chocolate (in moderation)
Seeds and Nuts	Ginseng and Peppermint

*As you read in item 6 above, turkey and eggs are linked to some nasty stuff so be sure your consumption of these two dopamine boosters are limited in order to reduce the risks noted above.

10. Regular cheese is one of the most dangerous foods in the world. Only eat low-fat cheese, and very small portions.

11. High fiber foods prevent cancer (but it must come from foods, not fiber supplements).

12. There are many huge benefits to eating broccoli.

13. People with cholesterol levels lower than 150 almost never have heart attacks.

14. Leafy greens are the most nutrient rich food that exists.

15. The best advice for life is to use no oil because of its high calorie content per tablespoon.

16. There are great benefits to fasting (fast for 1 to 2 days twice a month—water only).

17. Ground flax seeds are much better than flax seed oil.

18. Try to eat one pound of greens per day.

19. Try to eat 100 grams of natural fiber per day.

20. Eat lots of strawberries, blueberries, and melons—these are great anti-cancer food.

21. There are virtually no heart attacks for vegetarians or people who get 10% or fewer calories from animal product

22. Drink lots of water—1 1/2 to 2 liters per day.

23. Challenge yourself to try a six-week diet without any animal or diary products except for fish and Egg Beaters.

24. Don't buy or bring foods into your house that are not healthy. (Why tempt yourself?)

25. Leave trays or bowls of fresh fruit and vegetables out on your desk or kitchen counter.

26. Last, but not least, your life will be greatly empowered in everything you do if you firmly set goals for great health.

CHAPTER ELEVEN

The Elixir of Life: Gratitude

Nearly every one loves a celebration—regardless of age or country or culture. The kind of celebrating I'm talking to you about is not some mindless, wild party that is just an excuse for everyone to drink too much. That really doesn't do anyone much good.

**What I'm talking about is a
celebration of your accomplishments
(even the small ones) to give your life a jolt!**

Yes, a celebration to hotwire your passion for life. And, yes, during this celebration, there should be a good amount of toasting, in appreciation . . . of you.

Certainly a celebration is a good thing—right? But am I saying you should pat yourself on the back for a job well done in front of associates, friends, and family? Am I talking about thanking yourself and showing appreciation and giving gratitude . . . to you?

Isn't that a bit egotistical—a little vain, even over-the-top? Maybe, but it also has a certain honesty and intelligence to it. **Besides it's healthy to value . . . you.** (I'll talk about giving value and appreciation to others around you in a minute.)

The Two Sides of One Coin

No doubt we've all heard that we can't love and appreciate others until we truly love and appreciate ourselves.

But most of us have some deep dark doubts about ourselves. In fact, if we are brutally honest, we feel guilty (at least some of the time) because we know we've done things we are not proud of—and we think, "If the world really knew everything about me, it wouldn't think I was a very good person."

You've had those thoughts before, at least if you're normal. Rabbi Harold F. Kushner, in his book, *Living a Life That Matters*, makes that point very strongly by saying,

"Good people do bad things."

But he goes on to say,

"If they weren't mightily tempted by their 'yetzer hara' (evil inclination) they might not be capable of the mightily good things they do."

He then goes on to tell of the Native American tribal leader who describes his own inner struggles by saying, "There are two dogs inside me. One of the dogs is mean and evil. The other dog is good. The mean dog fights the good dog all the time."

Someone asked him which dog usually wins, and after a moment's reflection he answered, **"The one I feed the most."**

Kushner continued,

"Good people will do good things—lots of them, because they are good people. They will do bad things because they are human."

Celebrate the Good

So the bottom line here is even if you know you are not perfect, it's important to take time to toast and be grateful for the good things you've accomplished and those tough goals you've reached. Always remember the wise words of Rabbi Kushner and don't be so hard on yourself.

No one's perfect—not you, not me!

**So, start forgiving yourself now,
have a little gratitude (ditch the humility for a while),
and hey, why not make a toast about
putting all that guilt behind you.**

Focus on all the good you've done, and the new journey you are embarking on now and the good that will come from that. It will help feed the good dog inside of you. Remember this from the Dalai Lama's book, *The Compassionate Life*, where he said,

**"Everyone's real enemy is within
themselves—enemies are not on the outside."**

SO, WHY NOT CELEBRATE AND FEED THE GOOD DOG INSIDE YOU, OFTEN?

Now, be careful here. Celebrating and toasting yourself can be a life-enhancing experience. But just like with great wine and great food, you can easily overdo it, and that's not so good for you.

Celebrations, to make the most impact on you and to make a difference in your life, are better left for very special occasions—like when you stretch yourself and have reached a significant goal that you set. Can you imagine the joyous celebration for the two climbers, Joe Simpson and Simon Yates, when they finally made it off the frozen Peruvian mountain and back to safety and civilization? (See Chapter Six) Wow, just imagine the exhilaration, the gratitude for life and limb—and the wonderful reality that Joe was alive!

> **Focus on all the good you've done, and the new journey you are embarking on now and the good that will come from that.**

No, you and I don't have to almost die to celebrate life, but any close encounter with death that I've had certainly has intensified my celebrations and toasting of life.

Some people seem to have a fantastic knack of knowing just how to celebrate life. They know the perfect time and place. Then they take great care to make everything perfect for the celebration or event. If you're lucky enough to know those people and to be invited to participate, you know how much you look forward to that date in the future.

I'm in the center of this photo surrounded by some of the greatest friends a guy can have. We're at the *Annual Stein and Francoise Eriksen Tennis Tournament*. To my right is Eva Eriksen-Evans, then Francoise Eriksen, and Bjorn Eriksen. To my left is Stein Eriksen, my wife Kimberly, and Brian Evans.

Montana Mountain Toast

For example, my wife, Kimberly, and I look forward with great anticipation, all year long, to the last week in August when we attend a great celebration of friends at the Annual Stein and Francoise Eriksen Tennis Tournament. Stein Eriksen was the 1952 Olympic Gold Medalist of the Men's Giant Slalom. He also won the World Cup that year.

Stein was born and raised in Norway, but has lived in the United States since winning his Gold Medal. His wife, Francoise, was born and raised in Normandy, France. Their "annual tournament" is very much a celebratory event for their friends and loved ones that takes place annually at their Montana mountain retreat—and, oh, what a celebration!

To know why it is so wonderful, you've got to look at it closely. It's in the details. Everything from flowers, food, friends, and fun—plus, of course, tennis, trophies, and toasts. And believe you me, there are some wonderful and sincere toasts made. The Norwegians and the French certainly know how to celebrate.

The great lesson of life that the Eriksen's have learned is that of human interdependence. They raise their glasses, filled with wonderful French

134

wine, of course, during the "tournament" and give thanks and appreciation to the many, many people who have graced, charmed, and assisted them in living their lives.

**Without those friends, they say their
lives would certainly be very empty.**

Think about it—all events and incidents in your life are linked to other humans. Some you like, some may repulse you—but nevertheless, all are connected to your life.

To paraphrase the Dalai Lama, he says that our interdependence is a fundamental law of nature.

Human interdependence is a must because without a doubt other people are the principal source of our experiences of joy, happiness, and prosperity. A person alone cannot achieve anything—certainly not fulfillment. You can't even cheat without someone to cheat.

What a privilege to shake hands with His Holiness, the Dalai Lama during a recent visit to the United States. I credit the Dalai Lama's philosophy and teaching of human interdependence and the caring expression of compassion and gratitude for all humanity as a major influence on my life.

He goes on to wisely say that no matter how rich or independent you are, you must rely on others. Even the best and most expensive machine in the world can't give you love, tenderness, compassion, and appreciation. It would be interesting for you and I to see how we would feel if some preprogrammed machine or computer were to tell us how much "it" appreciated and loved us, and then asked a bunch of other machines to raise "their" glasses and make a toast to us. Hey, if the world comes to that sad point, I hope I'm "toast" by then.

You and I should take a page from the "Eriksen book" and plan celebrations for our own milestone achievements and other special occasions, taking the time to plan out the details of our "toast times" and really make them something special.

Here's one more added incentive.

■ **When you set major goals in your life, take the time right then to attach to those goals a written brief on how and what you're going to do to celebrate the reaching of that goal.**

It's one more B-RAM™ that will sweeten the victory of your own goal achievement. The process of writing it down gives your mind a wonderful boost as you look forward to that date in the future when you will toast your victory.

Your Own Annual Celebration Day

Now, take it one step further. Why not set up an Annual Goal Celebration Day, inviting those special people who have played a part in your life and success?

■ **Plan it well—you know—attention to the details.**

■ **Dovetail some of your goals to coincide with that date of your celebration day.**

In addition to being an extra incentive for you to reach your goal by that date, an Annual Goal Celebration Day can be such a great reminder to us of how precious and wonderful life is.

We need to relish it and appreciate it to the max.

During this Celebration Day, give awards for what we've accomplished for the year. That's right.

Give an award to yourself.

Be sure to also take the time and thought to include those many people who have been an influence and helped you by also acknowledging them.

Once again, to quote the Dalai Lama,

> **"The moment you think of others with a sense of caring . . . your view widens. Within that wider perspective, your own problems appear to be of little significance, and this makes a big difference."**

Isn't this at least part of the reason you feel so good when you raise your glass and say good things about someone else.

I know it's not easy or convenient to arrange and organize events to celebrate with your friends, family, and associates. If you are like me, while you are busting your butt preparing and organizing the event, you probably will start saying to yourself, "Wow, this is just not worth the effort."

However, again if you are like me, after the evening is over and everyone has gone home, you'll have this wonderful warm feeling of satisfaction and you'll say to yourself, "Wow, was that great and so well worth the effort."

So what are you waiting for?

Go start preparing for a big or small event to celebrate.

Do it now—and keep doing it with regularity!

You won't be sorry—it will lift your life as it lifts the lives of others around you.

As the Buddhists say,

"Live wisely selfish, as opposed to foolishly selfish."

Great Gratitude—Great Joy

As I'm sure you know—if not, I'm certainly going to tell you right now—

GRATITUDE IS PROBABLY THE
MAIN INGREDIENT FOR GREAT JOY.

Scientists tell us that whenever we show or express gratitude we apparently process the experience in the frontal region of our brain, which is the same region where "wonder and awe" are processed. The feel-good chemicals of dopamine and serotonin are very likely stimulated as a result of simple thoughts of gratitude.

So the bottom line is

**that the more you show and express gratitude,
not only does the receiver of your gratitude feel better,
but you (the giver) also feel better.**

Okay, maybe it's a bit selfish, but it's a wise selfishness rather than a foolish one—and it really works wonders. If you don't believe me let me prove it to you right now.

Go ahead and do the following and see how you feel. Grab a pen and write down in the space below all of the things, people, and events you are grateful for. Go ahead, do it right now.

For example, let me give you a list of just 10 things I quickly wrote down as items I am extremely grateful for:

1. Family—great kids and grandkids.

2. A fantastic, helpful, and loving wife.

3. Supportive and good friends.

4. People who've helped my life through their lives, their examples, and their books—many, many authors.

5. Good health.

6. The ability to move freely, without any pain.

7. A great tennis game yesterday with good friends.

8. A comfortable house with years of fantastic memories.

9. Good, healthy food.

10. Very talented, smart, and loyal associates and employees.

Now create your own list of about 20 things, people, and events you are grateful for:

_____

_____

_____

_____

_____

_____

_____

_____

Okay, now reread your list and think about it. Ask yourself, after you've finished, how it makes you feel reading about all those wonderful people and things or events in your life.

Gold Medal Gratitude

Gratitude for the contribution of others in our lives, our acknowledgment of their support, and giving credit for their part in our successes and triumphs, I believe, keeps you more humble, open, and more connected to "those who brought you to the dance." It serves as a slingshot for greater triumph and personal satisfaction.

> **Gratitude for the contribution of others in our lives, I believe keeps you humble.**

Let me give you an example from my own life by sharing with you my gold medal experience. I could not have done it without a bunch of support, inspiration, and help mainly from three great people.

I'm pictured (above) with the Gold Medal I won at the 2007 Huntsman World Senior Games in the Singles Tennis Competition. Although a medal was my goal when I entered the games, I could not have won it without the critical support of others: Dr. Harlan Amstutz, my hip replacement surgeon; Roy Emerson, my tennis coach; and Paul J. Meyer, my spaced repetition mentor and inspiration who still plays tennis at 80 years of age. These individuals and many other family members and friends are all connected to my triumph. I did not do it alone—I could not do it alone.

Each of us is connected to the many who support us in everything we accomplish. Giving them credit, acknowledgement, and our profuse gratitude is a sure-fire way to keep the triumphs coming.

I had a goal to reach the top of the tennis rankings in my state. I certainly worked at it. But I had a problem in the way of my goal. I was more and more unable to run, bend, or walk more than 200 yards without stopping because of the pain in my two arthritic hips. (See Movement Is a Must in Chapter 10, "An Umbrella Goal for LIFE") So how did I win the gold medal in the Men's 60-65 Singles Tennis Tournament at the 2007 Huntsman World Senior Games?

- **First, a ton of credit goes to Paul J. Meyer (www.success-motiva-ion.com or pauljmeyer.com) who taught me by word and example to never stop setting and going after goals—he preached over and over to me to do this all my life—no matter what. He also showed me the power of spaced repetition. What did that mean for me? It meant that I hit thousands and thousands of tennis balls. I wore out two ball machines in the process.**

- **Second, I owe a huge amount of credit to the one-time most winning tennis player in the history of tennis—the incomparable Australian Roy Emerson. He conducted a phenomenal one-week tennis camp high in the mountains of Switzerland (www.RoyEmersonTennisWeeks.com) that consisted of many long hours of teaching techniques, strategies, and drills that nearly wore my brand new hips to a frazzle. But what great lessons I learned!**

- **And third … about those new hips—WOW! Without those pieces of chromium cobalt placed so perfectly by a great surgeon with steady hands and many years of experience, the example and coaching of Paul J. Meyer and Roy Emerson would not have won me the gold. Dr. Harlan Amstutz of the Joint Replacement Institute (www.jri-docs.com) deserves so much thanks and credit for my tennis success. He gave me my young life back.**

Now about my goal of being in the top rankings for tennis in my state—as published on February 4, 2008 (www.tennislink.usta.com) I am the NUMBER ONE ranked tennis player in Utah, for my age group.

As you progress through your own life at every stage, whether you're just starting out or you're an old fart like me, be sure to fully realize that:

- **You owe so many for helping you along your success path.**

- **None of us, no matter how smart we think we are or even how lucky we may be, we cannot do it or go it alone.**

- **Take time to give credit and gratitude. It truly will amaze you how much joy and energy you will add to your life and everyone around you.**

Journal Your Journey

My great and longtime friend, Richard Harvey (we played basketball together in Ankara, Turkey, and also in the Olympic Stadium in Rome, Italy), graciously gave me the wonderful phrase,

"JOURNAL YOUR JOURNEY"

**Three great words to describe
what you're really doing by
listing what you're grateful for.**

By writing down what you're grateful for, including certain people, events, and lots of other things in your life, you begin the process of journaling your journey. The very process of recording your life completely, with your innermost thoughts, is an additional way to celebrate and make a "toast" to your life.

I highly recommend it.

Later, when you reread your own words, those words not only give a great perspective on your life, they can also give great inspiration and incentive to continue to set and achieve goals.

While I was writing this I picked up one of my old journals and read my entry on March 13, 1995, which gave me some great perspective (and by the way, I've kept a journal since February 16, 1964). My March 1995 read:

> "Yes, it did feel right—wrote a letter to Cammy—telling her how wonderful I thought she was—read most of my journal entries from 1964 to 1994. Wow, what a trip to read through thirty years of my life in three hours—to move so quickly through my thoughts and words as a twenty-year-old to a fifty-year-old in a matter of 180 minutes was to see one-third of my life zip by on fast forward.

It's scary to put it mildly. I shared some of my deepest thoughts with my daughter, Cammy. I think she'll understand that I hadn't planned on it, but when I write they just come out. I hope she understands me better. I hope I understand me better."

From rereading this just now, almost 14 years later, I got even more perspective of my life and it gave me even more motivation to do other meaningful things that will help other people's lives.

**What a great gift you'll be giving to your kids,
and your grandkids,
and your great, great, great-grandkids by
"journaling your journey."**

And as important, celebrate your life, your loves, your accomplishments, and the achievement of your goals. And don't forget to raise a glass often in heartfelt gratitude and toast your victories—and do it now (before you're toast).

CHAPTER TWELVE

The Benefits of a "God's-Eye View"

A few years ago I watched the two Williams sisters (Venus and Serena) duke it out in the Finals of England's famous Wimbledon Tennis Tournament. I couldn't help but put myself inside their father's head as he watched his two daughters battle hard, one trying to beat the other. All I could think about was that the only way Richard Williams could sit and watch the match was as if he were God. Obviously, he cared about both his daughters, and loved them both equally and deeply. He couldn't help but cheer for both of them—be proud of both of them. And, it probably didn't matter to him who won the match.

When you're a parent, you start learning the "God lesson" or you begin to develop a "God perspective" on many things—or what I call a "God's-Eye View" or simply GEV.

> **Having a GEV allows you to see both sides of most, if not all issues. You can rejoice with the winner and at the same time you share the pain of the loser.**

The more you develop a "God's Eye View" the easier it is to see another person's point of view and relate to their circumstances. With GEV you can more easily have compassion for not only the "other" guy, but for all of humanity.

GEV allows you to be:

■ **More open to everything going on around you,**

- To comprehend needs and motivations,

- To better serve others, even you giving without hesitation to total strangers—

- And especially being able to freely give back to a world that has so freely given to you.

Working on Your Own GEV

Working on yourself and your own GEV is so very rewarding. Many of you already know what I'm talking about. Others of you have an "inkling" or have experienced GEV, at least to some degree.

I want to do all I can
    to encourage—
        to motivate you—
            to work more on cultivating your own GEV.

Don't follow the old saying, "Give 'til it hurts."

Go for the more factual, accurate axiom,

"Give until your heart is so warm,
overwhelmed and full, that it's ready to burst."

But hey, have you ever wondered why you feel so good when you give like that to others and do kind deeds?

I wanted to know the answer to that question so I did a little research. I found that it has a lot to do with our chemistry.

It's Chemistry

Recent studies have proven that not only the recipient of a kind deed has a jump in their brain serotonin levels, but also the doer of that deed has an equal increase in brain serotonin and, hence, gets that rush of warm fuzzies running through their brain and body.

Now I don't want you to think I'm pushing the idea of "giving back to the world" for the sole purpose of seeing how much you can

get out of the deal. Quite frankly, I think that if a person were to approach "giving back" with that kind of motive, that their brain just might outfox them and refuse to release the necessary chemicals. **Parts of our brain, strangely enough, seem to be so much wiser and smarter than other parts of that same brain.**

It's About Caring

The God's Eye View can help you and me in many ways as it pulls us steadily and passionately toward giving of our time, our money, and ourselves to others, because we truly care.

Now here's a true test. What about your GEV when you lose at almost anything, whether it's a sporting event, a business deal, a great job opportunity, or even a big income tax battle with the IRS? In all those situations, when it would be so easy to get upset, GEV will effortlessly guide you to think this:

> **"Hey, everything is okay. I'm going to look at this from a God perspective—someone else won and I will be happy for them. They are just as important as I am, whether they are my child, my friend, a total stranger, or even my enemy. I will cheer for them now and be truly glad for them in their victory."**

Edging God Out

I have great sympathy for people who always have to win no matter what. They really have a problem. Continuing with that attitude and mindset will either kill them or at least make their lives absolutely miserable. **It's pretty much all about ego**—or as some wise person once proposed,

> **"EGO is 'Edging God Out.'"**

They are also losing out because they don't see the wonder and the great benefits of developing a true "God's Eye View" for their life and for the world.

Even if you don't believe in God, I hope you can see the beauty and the benefit of developing a GEV of the world in every single aspect of your life, whether it be business or personal.

With a heavy dose of GEV you can become a huge "giver" and help lift the world to a higher level. And even though it was not your primary motivation, you will realize huge personal rewards. Rewards that you never heretofore dreamt were possible.

Try it—
Test it—
Prove it by doing it!

I dare you! I certainly know from personal experience when I do it, I'm always stunned, amazed, impressed, so much so that I want to do it again and again.

The Hindu Perspective

Maybe you're not ready for all this giving and all this altruism, and you're not doing it now and don't want to, because it simply does not appeal to you. People who follow the Hindu philosophy and religion would basically say, "Hey, that's okay . . . wait until it comes to you, wait until it speaks to you . . . then it will be time to do it."

So if you're not ready to give back to the world, that's okay. Or maybe you just want to start very slowly and see how it feels.

My good friend Paul J. Meyer is approaching $60 million in his "giving program."

But for me, and countless others, his biggest gift has been his example and his words of wisdom found in his dozens of books, tapes, and CDs. What an enormous contribution he has made to the world. (Check him out at www.pauljmeyer.com)

Then there is the powerful example of multi-billionaire Jon Huntsman, Sr. I've known Jon for many years—I even knew him when he was poor or at least before he hit it really big. And, yes, he was just as giving when he didn't have two nickels to rub together.

Now those nickels have turned into billions and he's given away about a quarter of a billion dollars—given it back to the world, and he's not even close to being done.

148

Here are just a few of his favorite causes:

1. **Huntsman Cancer Institute**

2. **Huntsman World Senior Games**

3. **Huntsman Awards for Excellence in Education (Annually giving 10 teachers $10,000 each)**

4. **Annual Gifts (Varied gifts to homeless shelters and sanctuaries for abused women and children)**

5. **American Red Cross**

6. **Wharton School of Finance**

You might want to pick up Jon Huntsman, Sr.'s great little book entitled, *Winners Never Cheat*. It's a marvelous read and one that will lift your ethical life to a much greater height.

Some Just Don't Get It

It's incredible to me that so many people just don't get it—they not only fail to realize the gigantic benefits to everyone (including themselves) from "giving back." Some of these same people get even greedier after having received huge windfalls. Take the Enron executives situation of a few years ago, for example. ("Google" it if you don't know what happened.) Here $100 million wasn't enough, so they had to lie, steal, and cheat to make twice that much. **I'm pretty sure that those kinds of actions and behaviors will suck any and all pleasure, contentment, and life out of anyone, and probably totally drain the serotonin tank to empty.**

How about Richard Hatch? Do you remember him? He became known as the "fast naked guy" on the CBS *Survivor* series for refusing to wear any clothes. I never watched the show, but I couldn't help seeing the newspaper coverage when he won $1 million dollars at the end of the show's season. Later, it became obvious that he wasn't very grateful and apparently had not a clue about the so-called GEV.

> **People fail to realize the gigantic benefits to everyone (including themselves) from "giving back."**

Why do I think that? Well, it has something to do with Mr. Hatch currently sitting in federal prison in Oklahoma. It seems that he not only didn't give back to the world, but he failed to pay taxes on the million dollars he won. Then, to top it all off, according to the judge, he repeatedly lied on the witness stand.

**What do you think was happening to
Richard Hatch's internal chemistry
as he was lying to the court?**

Not only did his serotonin levels most likely nosedive, the affect on his body at the cellular level must have been disastrous.

Lies are toxic to the body, as is,

■ **stealing,**

■ **hoarding,**

■ **and cheating.**

Buffet's Billions

On the other hand, imagine what goes on in your own body and mind when you give freely, and without strings, to your children and family, to your friends, associates, and even to total strangers?

Do you think, for example, something very good started happening inside Warren Buffet's mind and body when in mid-2006 he began giving away the majority of his billions?

> **Developing a "God's Eye View" could possibly produce more powerful health-giving and healing benefits than modern medicine or prescription drugs.**

He also strongly refused that his name be put on any edifice or institutions—he didn't even set up Buffet Scholarships or a Buffet Endowment Fund.

It's my opinion, if scientists were able to completely measure all that goes on inside the human body, from the cells to levels of serotonin, I believe they would find that developing a "God's Eye View" and practicing it and giving freely to the world, these GEV thoughts and actions alone would produce more powerful health-giving and healing benefits than modern medicine or prescription drugs.

If You Don't Have Billions

But hey, if you don't happen to have a few extra million to spread around to make the world a better place, listen to what Ralph Waldo Emerson said (not a bad source of some great wisdom for all ages):

> **"To know that even one life has breathed easier because you have lived—that is to have succeeded."**

There are so many ways to give to the world. Yes, some of those ways are big-time and grandiose, while others are so very plain and simple—even small.

One of my favorite quotes is what Mother Teresa said,

> **"There are not great deeds, just small deeds done with great love."**

Never forget that. The real foundation of giving back, in my opinion, is your inner attitude and what lies really deep down inside your heart.

Studying to Give at 37,000 Feet

On my way to Paris to celebrate with my staff the super-successful completion of our Hawaiian development, my wife and I couldn't help but notice a giant of a man engrossed in his book. Who was this almost 7-foot guy, and what was he reading? I was very surprised to learn that this Latvian basketball player was studying his own country's history. Why? So he could give back to the world.

Kaspars Kambala was filling his brain with the lessons learned from the experiences and lives of his countrymen. As he later explained to me, many people had asked him about his country, but to his embarrassment, he had not been able to answer their questions because he had not paid attention while in school.

Now, he was determined to learn all he could so that when people asked, he could describe his country's rich history, thereby enriching others' lives.

At age 27, he told me he was really at a crossroads and was truly getting serious about his life and what he could do with it. He had already done some pretty incredible things—from playing professional basketball at the tender age of 15 in Latvia—to moving by himself to the U.S. where he played college basketball at the University of Nevada—then moving to Turkey, he won the 2001–02 and 2002–03 Turkish National Championships. His team also won the 2002 Turkish National Cup. Now he plays for Fenerbahce Ulker, a professional basketball team that is part of the Euroleague (visit: www.euroleague.net).

> **A dignified and long-lasting influence can do more good in your world than millions of dollars in cash aid.**

I'd say he had had a pretty full life already. But now, as we flew at 37,000 feet, he was thinking even higher. I certainly was impressed with his ambition, but even more so with his attitude. Here was a gentle giant, who not only cared deeply about his wife and child, but also about his country and becoming a self-appointed ambassador to all people of the world. His dignified, long-lasting influence will likely do more good for his country abroad than millions of dollars in cash aid.

As You Do, You Do to You

So, if you are in that place, and if it feels right to you now—if you're ready to give back—go ahead and begin. And know this, as my good friend, Joe Land, is fond of saying:

"As you do, you do to you."

A few weeks ago, I was asked by an old friend to come to federal court for her husband's criminal sentencing. She needed some moral support. I went, a bit reluctantly, but for friendship, I just had to go.

Her husband had admitted his guilt and then made a deal with the court in exchange for leniency. But he failed to deliver on his promise and held back hundreds of thousands of dollars that were to go to some of his victims. He wouldn't surrender the money—he was holding on to it for dear life, which actually cost him his life—or at least five years of it, for that was the length of his sentence.

I think his failure to surrender the money was just the tip of the iceberg. His strong, tough-guy, know-it-all, non-surrendering resistance (that I'm pretty sure will continue for the next five years) could very well "do him in" permanently. What could save him?

> **The same thing that can save all of us and make all our lives so much better—and that is to develop a strong sense of GEV and surrender ourselves to good causes, to do what we know is good for the world.**

This man, who was going to prison, knew and admitted his guilt, but wouldn't give back to those he owed, which set up the totally wrong mind-set for his prison stay, and will most likely make those five years miserable, even a living hell. **Not only had he cheated others, he had cheated himself.**

But it could be so much different for him. If he were willing and would surrender to a GEV, he could make those five years a huge personal victory.

- **With a strong resolve to better himself and the world around him, he could start paying back and fulfilling his promise to return all the money.**

- **With very few distractions while in prison, he could also study hard and learn all that he possibly could about almost any subject under the sun. In five years he could be an expert. And if that subject were one that could help humanity, even all the better.**

- **He could also get himself in topnotch shape both physically and mentally.**

The bottom line: he could use those five years to come out of prison as a new, improved man, ready to make a difference in the world—for good.

The Same Opportunity

You and I have that same opportunity. In the next five years, without losing our freedom (and maybe with a few more distractions than if we were sitting alone in prison), we can set whatever goals we want to achieve and to accomplish. We can become and do what we truly want to do. I hope we'll never lose that perspective. I hope that we'll always remember we are all in this world together, and the "God's Eye View" should tell us that in many ways there is only one of us here.

WE ARE ALL THAT ONE HUMAN BEING.

Horrific tragedies, like what happened on September 11, 2001, teach us that lesson with powerful emotion. Who can recall or watch any reenactment or documentary or movie about that day without tearing up and feeling such loss for those who died, and feel such compassion and empathy for their families and friends.

And yet, the vast majority of us didn't lose a single loved one or even a friend. Why do we feel these strong feelings? I think there are three reasons:

1. **Those people were totally innocent**

2. **Each of us can put ourselves in their place, and**

3. **All of those people who died were a part of us (which I think is the biggest reason of all).**

This was so beautifully illustrated through the story of two French filmmakers, the brothers Gedeon and Jules Naudet, who were filming near the World Trade Center that fateful morning. Quite by accident they caught on film the first plane as it crashed into the north tower. Then a short time later, they were running for their very lives away from the collapsing building. Having lost each other in the chaos, each brother thought the other one had died.

Later, when they were reunited, they said it was so euphoric and deeply emotional that it was like they had seen each other for the first time after years of separation, even though their separation had been but a few hours.

Even more surprising to the brothers was the depth of emotion and feelings for and bond they felt with the firemen they had been filming and working with (Engine 7, Ladder 1 of the New York Fire Department) that day. Even though they did not know them intimately, as they did each other, they felt strongly the loss of all 50 firefighters from this station. It was as if they had truly been their brothers!

Because of their life-changing experience, it did not surprise me to read just last week that these two brothers, Gedeon and Jules, are doing a film entitled, *In God's Name.* It's about the Dalai Lama, a man whose life and beliefs echo compassion, kindness, and the oneness of all humans.

If you think deeply about it, you will see that not only were those 50 men their brothers, but everyone who lives and breathes on this earth is also a part of them. Literally, everyone who has ever lived, who has taken a breath and then exhaled, their DNA has become a part of us, as you and I have inhaled their essence with each breath we take—thus uniting us all.

Our passion for living takes on a much more universal feel through a God's Eye View. To give freely, to love without hesitation or qualification, and to become the absolute best you can be, is a gift to all of us. It is how we can lift and affect the entire world—for good.

**Never forget—there's only one of us here,
AND
we are ALL that one person.**

CHAPTER THIRTEEN

The GREATEST Lesson of LIFE

I'm closing this book with the promise I opened with:

> **Is there a sure-fire path you can follow to ensure that you reach each goal, every time you set one? You will clearly see as you read this book that the answer is an emphatic, 'YES!' I'll show you exactly how this is done. I know you can do it. I know this because I've done it . . .**

Here's the key. This is how I've reached almost every goal that I've set. (Burn this into your brain—it has been burned in mine.)

I GET GOING, RIGHT THEN!

- **ACTION, right at the moment I've set the goal.**

- **NO waiting for later.**

- **NO waiting for better timing.**

- **NO way. I get going right away.**

The most beautifully conceived and written goals are not worth the paper they are written on if I don't immediately and methodically spring into action, holding nothing back.

Doing this, I've experienced great fulfillment, achievement, and passion in my life. By springing into action the moment you resolve to do so, I promise you that a flood of passion will flow into your your life, and the kind of fulfillment and passion that very few people ever experience.

The Greatest Lesson

In the first part of this book I told you of some of the great tragedies that transformed my life. They were truly devastating. But it was that very devastation that jolted me and demanded that I live life more fully—grasping for more moments of joy and more life out of my life.

**It made me appreciate and love more than
I probably ever would have without those tragic jolts.**

Recently, my wife and I traveled to Switzerland to spend some more of those precious moments visiting my very dear Swiss friends, the Moros (Marco, Chris, Reto, Eva, Jasmin, and Ana). During those few relaxing days in Switzerland I reacquainted myself with a marvelous and tragic story I had read about many years before.

Perhaps you may remember it, too? It was the subject of a TV documentary, a movie, and a book, all entitled *Alive*. It is the story about a plane that crashed on a glacier high in the Andes. The Fairchild aircraft was carrying members of the Uruguayan Rugby Team to a match in Chile. Along for the ride were friends and family. On impact many of the 45 passengers on board were killed, and others died within days, while still others died later from exposure or starvation. A few more died weeks later when an avalanche raced down the mountain during the night. Only 16 survived and did so by eating the flesh of their dead teammates. They somehow miraculously stayed alive for a total of 72 days and nights with temperatures dropping well below zero.

> **Life must be lived every day—every moment—and with every breath, with the greatest gusto and pounding passion that you can muster.**

A new book, *Miracle in the Andes*, is a fresh look at the ordeal faced by the survivors, from the unique perspective of one of the survivors. And what a story it is, with a powerful life-changing and life-enhancing message. The most profound miracle and life-altering message of this tragic story that hit me square over the head and in my gut was that life must be lived every day—every moment—and with every breath, with the greatest gusto and pounding passion that you can muster. (Yes, you've heard that before—especially in this book)

Nando Parrado, the author of this new book, was one of the two young men who eventually walked, climbed, and crawled for 11 days to civilization and sent a rescue party. In the book, he shares his most intimate thoughts and feelings as he faced almost certain death, and he writes in such a vivid and open way that the message of living each moment, and the critical importance of giving love and being loved, resonates in the human mind like none other that I've ever read.

Nando also put his incredible experience into words in such a way that I think it will inspire and motivate me to never forget what we tend to forget so very often. Nando indicated something that I have held true ever since the death of my daughter, Kristin.

What Nando revealed was:

"There may be only one good thing that can come from great human tragedy, and that is tragedy can make you so much more human than you ever were before."

With no experience or equipment, Nando Parrado and a companion climbed over one of the highest peaks in the Andes Mountains, a grueling 11-day trek to civilization, and the ultimate rescue for all the crash survivors.

Being more human influences you and me to care more about other human beings.

- ■ **It teaches you and me to be more aware and empathetic of other people's problems and tragedies . . .**

- ■ **to cry and hurt for other people in their losses, even people you don't know.**

- ■ **At other times it teaches you to rejoice and celebrate their triumphs.**

Maybe that's why this extreme human empathy that I've felt has caused me to conclude that there really is only one of us here on this planet.

This is a photo of the actual rescue of the survivors, taken from the helicopter as it landed. Nando Parrado was on the helicopter to ensure that they found the wreckage. He refused medical treatment until all were safely rescued. Nando lost over 80 pounds during his 72-day ordeal. Although extremely weak, yet determined, the last 10 days of the ordeal, he and a companion climbed over the summit and down the mountain to civilization.

You Are in Control of Your Own Destiny, Breath By Breath

Since we are all part of this sea of humanity here on our planet, then it follows that the whole of humanity is advanced by the sum of its parts.

**This belief motivates me to take more responsibility
and seize more control over my life and
my own destiny for the good of the whole.**

A healthy self-interest and appetite for self-improvement thus makes a difference for the whole world.

Perhaps some people see this way of living and looking at your place in this world as pushing God out of the equation.

**But maybe that's exactly what God is—the power
to make a difference, to improve, to change
by exerting and useing our own free will.**

Many pious believers just sit back and pray that God will do it or deliver them or save them. And many others feel that whatever happens in their lives is God's will.

But what about what we will for our own lives?

The older I get, the more I believe that God is that overall force—a powerful feeling of good. The more experience I have in life, the more difficult it is for me to see God as a micromanager of people's lives. A God that listens to billions of prayers and says yes to some and no to others or a God that saves some people from dying in a plane crash and lets others walk away makes no sense to me! I see God more ultimately leaving the

> **Each of us will have to choose whether or not we contribute to or take away from humanity and the world.**

day-to-day living to each of us, to choose the course we will take in life, whether or not we contribute to or take away from humanity and the world—that is our choice.

**When I look at the whole of this world,
I see the basic good in the vast majority of people.**

But then I also see some who do very stupid or very destructive things because they're convinced that their God is the only true God or their particular brand of religion is the only true religion.

I find it difficult to believe such a God would condone depravity or give an exclusive franchise to one group of "chosen people." In my mind it is totally illogical, because many times, what some mete out in the name of God is destructive to humanity. (Thus, I believe, eventually destructive to them.)

If you stop and analyze these "only true God" and "only true religion or church" claims, I think you can see how a person's ego is involved and how self-satisfying it is for them to think that they themselves are God's special people—that's a pretty powerful ego trip.

Making the Most

There are those who think that tragedy makes a person believe more or become closer to God. But that's not necessarily the truth. For me and many others I've met along my life's path, this is absolutely not the case. Yes, great tragedy can make one much more human, more caring. It can also make one bitter and hateful.

But, for me,

- **I've felt the power of tragedies, difficulties, and trials moving me toward being more teachable,**

- **and much more open to giving and receiving love,**

- **and much more open to the sea of humanity that stands with open arms willing to support me—and you.**

And this is where God may enter into the equation most, as this overall force for goodness and love.

Self-Honesty

Being more human and exerting my individual will, at least for me, has also meant being brutally honest with myself. It forced me to confront myself and challenge everything I believe and to constantly monitor and make sure it's my belief, not what an institution may be trying to persuade me to believe in. I also realize how much I don't know and therefore how I must be flexible in my thinking and beliefs and be willing to let the world and my experience teach me new ways of seeing life.

> **It seems to me that much of the world's problems**
> **are caused by rigid beliefs and thinking and**
> **the overall philosophy or belief that "we are the chosen,**
> **everybody else is frozen, and we're here to thaw them out."**

Nando's Lesson for Life

Nando Parrado's near death experience and 72 days of suffering physically, mentally, and emotionally (his mother and sister both died on the mountain) was very unique—especially in the great lesson it taught him about life. Even though he deeply respected the faith of his friends, he didn't share their heightened belief in God in the face of tragedy or at least in the same way.

Some of his friends were absolutely convinced during their ordeal that their only hope was that God would save them. And they sat there, waiting for that to happen.

> ## But Nando never believed that.

> **He was convinced that they would**
> **ultimately have to save themselves.**

It was that belief that drove him and a companion to the near impossible task of climbing alone over a 17,000 foot peak—a task that even professional climbers would not attempt without all the right support team and equipment, including pitons, ice-screws, safety ropes, etc., and weeks of precise planning. He and his companion made it to civilization, and sent help for the rest.

I, too, respect everyone's "God belief" as long as they don't use God as an excuse to hurt others or try to push their beliefs on me. But it seems to me that far too many sit back and wait for God to tell them what to do or help them achieve what they want their lives to be. They pray so earnestly and so hard to be saved, rather than using their own will and "God-given" abilities to find their own way over the many dangerous and difficult ice-covered passes of life.

You and I must decide where we sit in this matter. Am I "the captain of my own soul" and of my own life and of my own destiny—or am I adrift in a current of what others believe. Am I waiting for God to do it for me—or to manifest his will in my life. What about my will? Do I believe in my own power to push toward what I (REALLY) want.

I challenge you to live life fully, on your own terms.

**Constantly challenge yourself,
and fully give yourself to life, and to love,
and to the betterment of yourself and humanity.**

Enjoy every moment of life—cherish each breath—savor each sunset—and treasure each moment and each person who graces your path along the way.

The really tricky part for me of a living life passionately is that I must always be setting goals and pushing myself to reach them. But I have learned that true satisfaction comes in the journey along the way, treasuring each moment, and living in and enjoying the now—or as Nando Parrado promised himself, as he was wholly focused on his goal of getting over the mountain and to civilization, as death stalked him each step he took:

"I made a promise to myself. I would live from moment to moment and from breath to breath, until I had used all the life I had."

Live then, every moment.

Live by Nando's credo as you strive toward your dreams and goals—and experience abundant passion for life and living in this moment—and the next.

END NOTE
TO THE READER

I sincerely hope that this book has ignited your passion for living. And, as you apply the concepts and principles to your life, that each and every day will be greatly and permanently enhanced.

After this book has simmered for a short time, use the "spaced repetition" principle and re-read it. Once internalized, then *spring into action*.

If you want to *pass on the passion* and put this book in the hands of those whom you care about, please ***contact my office directly to order extra copies of this book at highly discounted prices.***

These prices are not available through regular distribution outlets, but only available from me . . . *to you*.

See the contact information and discounts on the last printed page of this book.

ADDENDUM A

Winning the Money Game Without Being Devoured By It

by Mark O. Haroldsen

I know very few people who are not looking to make more money.

We all see some pretty crazy things done by people so they can make lots of money. Sadly, some people will even kill for it—others take horrendous risks to make it multiply faster, while others totally turn their back on it as if it was the epitome of evil.

What is this thing we call money? Is it the sinister and evil force that some claim, or is it the greatest and most powerful force known to mankind?

Should we pursue money with all the energy and focus we can muster? And, when is enough, enough? Do we ever reach that point of making enough? Will tons of money make us feel secure and/or happy and content or is money, as a security blanket, an illusion?

We've all read about the billions of Bill Gates and Warren Buffet and wondered if making tons of money is worth the effort. We may even ask, does it ruin people's lives or enhance them? Obviously, it can do both. Is the love of money really the root of all evil, or is it something good? How do we earn a bunch of money without it devouring us? We've also read about the crooks of the world, the Ken Lays of Enron and others—the ones who got sucked in by their own greed glands. I believe there is something drastically wrong with a person's mind that thinks $200 million isn't enough and then conspires and cheats to turn it into $400 million—but it doesn't have to be that way.

With all this as a backdrop, I thought it would be very helpful to dig deep into the money game. Why? Well, because I think if we understand what money is and what it really isn't, that understanding can speed up the playing of the money game and make sure we win it without being devoured by it.

The young and inexperienced just want to get on with the winning of the game, as fast as they can. That's the real and only challenge they face. Yes, the enthusiasm and energy of youth is terrific; however, too many times they go off half-cocked—they don't take the time to learn the rules—and maybe even more importantly, they (and about half the rest of us) don't realize the huge pit that can be waiting for the financially successful.

In fact, a strong case can be made that the winning of the money game is the simple part compared to learning how not to be devoured by the game. The graveyards, the psych wards, drug addicts, and many devastated relationships can all attest to that fact.

Okay, so what is this thing called money and how important is it really? The modern day philosopher, Jacob Needleman, says that you have to face the money question, no matter what you do in life. And because money enters into every aspect of everyone's life, it has become more important to us than any other culture in history.

It can lift us to great heights of freedom, travel, pleasure, luxury, and influence. But, it also can deceive us into thinking that it is much more than it really is.

We all know that, at its very base, money is simply a medium of exchange. You could accurately say that money is stored up accomplishments of your work effort and energy, made negotiable. Whereas all that is true, the key to winning the money game (defining "winning" as amassing enough money so that the passive income you receive from that money sustains your desired lifestyle) is again very basic.

At the very base of winning is:

1) discipline,

2) simple mathematics (compounding),

3) an average dose of common sense.

In point of fact, that's all you need. All the rest—the fancy formulas, methods and financial systems—is the superstructure. Yes, the superstructure is valuable, but the base for that superstructure is absolutely, unquestionably the most critical part of the structure.

You see, if you consistently exercise discipline to always spend less money than you earn, and if you put what's left over of that money to work (regardless of the size) even at a moderate compound rate, you can literally turn a few thousand dollars into millions given enough years. It really is that simple!

The common sense part of the formula is simply applied by using your head to pick the secure investments that provide an acceptable yield with a relatively low risk.

> Example: Each $5,000 that you invest at 15% annual return will grow into 2.5 million dollars in 45 years—consequently, $10,000 will grow into 5 million in the same period of time, and $20,000 will grow to $10 million. Increase the rate and you obviously shorten the time period necessary for the same money. It's simple math, and it works every time.

However, the biggest problem we all face is that it's so easy to get sidetracked or lost because of the smoke and the mirrors that the media, the neighbors, and dozens of so-called financial gurus inadvertently throw at us from time to time. The smoke and mirrors are the misconceptions and the myths that surround money and there are lots of them.

Let me give you just a few of the many money myths:

1. Money is the root of all evil, so one should not pursue it.

2. To amass large amounts of money, you must be dishonest.

3. Making money is a zero-sum game. In a zero-sum game, every time you win or make money, someone loses and ends up with the same amount of money lost as you have gained.

4. You could never have too much money. Interpretation: no one could ever be totally satisfied with what they have.

5. If you have enough money, you'll automatically feel important and feel secure.

6. After you make a fortune, then your life will really begin.

7. Money is the most important thing in the world.

There's no question that money is a very powerful force and money can give you at least some feeling of security, but you'll never feel totally secure no matter how much money you have. It is common, for example, that, after some make tons of money, they feel even less secure because they worry about losing it. Security and feeling important is found by looking inward and through self-analysis and a self-discovery.

Yes, money is very powerful and can be life changing, but for those who think it is the most important thing and pursue it with that in mind—that is what will end up being the very thing that devours them.

We've all heard it said that "the joy really is in the journey, it's not in the destination" and that saying is more than the saying, "the journey is in actuality where the fun and the fulfillment are found."

You see, the key to not being devoured by money is really understanding the myths about money, especially myths 4, 5, 6, and 7 above. So, take time to study them and truly internalize them so when you make your fortune, using your definition of what a fortune is, you will not be devoured by the very thing that you pursued.

Resolve to enjoy the journey. Don't believe any of the above myths about money. Let money enhance your life by giving you more freedom and then use that freedom to get into the meaningful things of life. Enjoy the sun, the sand, and the sunsets. Truly inspire and invigorate your life with great music and art. Give of yourself in meaningful ways. Help people learn what you've learned. Appreciate what you have, as you acquire it, even if you're starting from a very small base, and mostly, as you strive toward your goals, and after you reach them, give back. Then give back some more so that you will win the money game and not be devoured by it.

ADDENDUM B

Curt Carlson Advice— When a Billionaire Speaks, I Listen

by Mark O. Haroldsen

More than 30 years ago *Fortune* magazine ran a story on "The Last of the Billionaires" that talked about how five different billionaires made their money.

I read the article very carefully, every word of that story, because I was very interested in how they did it. When I wrote "Goals, Guts & Greatness," I boldly stated on page 135 that I thought *Fortune* was dead wrong. They had concluded that we'd seen the last of the billionaires because of the tax laws and various other factors that would stop others from acquiring that sum of money now or in the future.

You see, one of the reasons I disagreed is because by then I was personally being coached by a billionaire by the name of Curtis Carlson.

In addition to our talks on the phone and meeting him on one of his cruise ships, I flew to Minneapolis for more coaching and a huge shot in the arm of motivation.

Here's what I said, followed by Curt Carlson's advice to me as I put it in "Goals, Guts & Greatness":

> "*Fortune* magazine suggests that we've seen the last of the billionaires. But I disagree. I feel that the human will is powerful enough to achieve even that great goal, if the desire and motivation are great enough. If a man can set a goal to make a million dollars and accomplish it, he can set a goal to make $10 million, or $100 million, and accomplish it. Why can't he go for a full billion?
>
> "Now, I'm not recommending that you set your goal to be a million-aire, or a billionaire—unless that's what you really want. What I am rec-

171

ommending is that you believe in yourself enough to set a high goal. Then, formulate your game plan, just as these billionaires did. Combine that with enough motivation and determination to execute the game plan and hit that goal.

"Believe in yourself enough to take the steps required to achieve whatever goal you set. If you can do that, you can reach—and exceed—your every dream."

Here's some of the advice that Curt Carlson gave me that day in Minneapolis way back then. He attributed his superior success to this advice, and notice as you read it that it's just as pertinent today as when he said it more than 20 years ago.

Carlson's Advice

"After you've got yourself going and have met your first goals," Curt Carlson said, "There are two things you should do to obtain super success."

"First," he said, "get the very best people you can find to help you reach your goals. Especially, find the best attorney and the best accountant that money can buy—and use them."

"Second, learn to delegate well. Don't try to do everything yourself. Match the right people with the right jobs and then give them the power of authority they need to carry out their responsibilities."

This advice may seem to be relatively insignificant. In fact, I myself might not have paid too much attention to it—if it weren't for the fantastic record that Curt Carlson has behind him.

He started with nothing 40 years ago. Even way back in 1981, his companies were privately held but exceeded one billion dollars in assets. Do you think Curt Carlson believed in his goals? The game plan? Motivation and determination? Action? Himself?

One last word about Curtis Carlson, whose fortune was in the multi-billions when he finally passed away a few years ago. This last word says it all.

In my first face-to-face meeting with him he was so very proud to pull out of his wallet a tattered piece of paper with his very first written goal on it. And that goal was to make $100 in a single week—yes, Mr. Carlson truly started at the very bottom and rose to the rarified air of a multi-billionaire.

Fortune certainly had it all wrong. They didn't know of the driving spirit of Mr. Curtis Carlson and the many others who are following him. There are now an estimate of about 500 billionaires in the world.

ADDENDUM C

Paul J. Meyer:
A *Life* to Pattern
Your *Life* After

by Steve Osborne

To look at Paul J. Meyer today—the ultra-successful owner of over 20 businesses, and the man who has sold more personal development courses, audio products, and booklets than any other living author—you would never guess that he was raised in a garage and spent most of his youth as a migrant worker.

Truth is stranger than fiction, and the truth about this entrepreneur's life would make a novel of Dickensian proportions.

"I came from very, very, very humble beginnings," says Paul. "My father was a carpenter and my mother was a school teacher. We lived in California, and we lived in a garage for 10 years. Times were hard. I worked with migrant farmworkers from the time I was 6 years old until I was 16. No one in our family had any formal education beyond high school, although we all eventually became educated through self-teaching." Paul now holds a handful of honorary doctorates from leading universities, plus a special degree from Baylor University.

After serving in the military, Paul began selling insurance in 1948 and quickly became a top producer, leading two of the nation's largest life insurance companies. He had acquired a personal net worth of $1 million by the age of 27. In 1958, Paul became a sales executive with a Waco, Texas, firm called Word, Inc., a company that distributed religious books and records, and increased its business by 1,500 percent by building an effective, motivated national sales organization.

In 1960, Paul founded the company with which his name has become associated: Success Motivation Institute, Inc. The company, which distributed motivational records at first, was and is dedicated to *motivating people to their full potential*. The product line quickly expanded to include Paul's full-length programs on motivation, leadership development, sales training, and management training. These programs include printed materials and audios, and are produced in over 20 languages for distribution to more than 60 countries of the world.

In addition, Paul has been a featured speaker throughout the United States, and has undertaken foreign tours in Asia, Europe, Australia, New Zealand, Canada, and South America. His success has been so notable (and beneficial to others because of his charitable instincts) that his city of residence—Waco, Texas—declared a special "Paul J. Meyer Day."

I'm visiting Paul J. Meyer (standing) at his beachfront retreat in the Cayman Islands. The photo that I'm holding is of Paul recording audios for the company he founded, Success Motivation Institute. SMI® currently markets success-oriented audios and books in the U.S. and in more than 60 countries with combined sales exceeding $2 billion, worldwide.

Light on His Feet

Although Paul owns numerous companies that are located all over the world and has several thousand employees around the globe, he has no official office.

"I have a president in charge of each of the companies," he explains. "Each president gives me a report at the end of each month. We compare the actual figures with the budget, with the goal, and with the previous year's figures so we know how we're doing. I only meet with each of them approximately once a quarter. I operate everything with a telephone, a fax machine, and e-mail."

Many business experts claim that businesses do not survive—let alone prosper—when the owner turns over the scepter of control to someone else and merely checks in to make sure that things are going well. Paul has proven that such an entrepreneurial system can work, and work well.

The secret? "You have to select and recruit top people," Paul explains. "I look for people that have the skill, the education, and the ability to do an excellent job. The man who runs our printing company knows 50 times more about printing than I do. Trust me, I couldn't carry his brief-case. And then, one of the most important things is the compatibility factor. How do they relate to people? How do they get along with people? How do they communicate with people?

"The number one thing that we look for in a person is character. They have to have character, integrity, and a good attitude."

A Book Gives Birth to a $100 Million Portfolio

Real estate has been one of Paul's key wealth-building tools.

"The first time I saw an ad for Mark Haroldsen's book, *How to Wake Up The Financial Genius Inside You*, I sent for it," recalls Paul. "According to his ad, I saw that we had a lot in common. We both started with nothing and used our God-given potential, and our desire, drive, determination, and positive attitude to do something. I didn't know anything about the real estate business. Nothing. When I got the book, I told my son, Larry, 'Why don't we take a run at it?'"

Their first "run" was the purchase of a rental house. Paul could have hired someone to fix up and maintain the house (he was extremely busy with other successful businesses at the time), but he knew that if he and Larry were going to stay in the business, they needed to know it from the ground level up. He acquired this attitude from his father, a German immigrant who told him to always take the time to be an apprentice first. Says Paul, "Our way of learning it was hands-on. We cleaned the bathtubs and the toilets. We painted it. We still own it. We'll never sell it. It's sort of a monument to us. In fact, it's paid for now, and we've put it in a trust for my son's third child."

Paul is a fast learner and doesn't let the moss grow under his feet when he knows what he wants. Not long after purchasing that first rental home, he bought another, and another, usually paying about 20 percent down.

"We ended up buying over 100 homes and over 50 duplexes in Waco, and a whole series of condos down in Austin. Then we started with small apartment complexes, and grew into the larger ones. We just kept growing."

"A lot of people suffer from the paralysis of analysis," says Paul. "Where I've been successful is that somewhere along the line I say, 'That's enough study, let's take a chance!' You've got to stick your neck out."

"We built our portfolio up all the way to $100 million in real estate. In fact, we ended up being about the largest landowners in two counties. Since then we've sold and sold and sold, and yet we still own approximately half of it. We have a whole ton of it now that's paid for, because we took the positive cash flow and applied it on the back. We still buy properties now, but we'll only buy them if they'll amortize in 10 to 15 years."

Paul claims that buying and selling real estate was and continues to be a business activity of exceptional excitement and enjoyment for him. "I enjoyed making the deals and negotiating," he states. "We didn't hire somebody else to do it. We looked at every single one of those properties personally—inside out, forward and backward." Within the past year, Paul purchased a building from a troubled bank. When someone called him to see if he was interested, he said that he wasn't, but that he'd go look at it. He walked through it, looked at the numbers, found that it was half empty and that it would cost three times more to build it than what he could buy it for, and purchased it on the spot. It didn't take him long to fill it up with renters after assuming ownership. The building was soon producing a positive cash flow and would be paid for in only six years.

Staying on Top of It All

In a world where owning a business is the quickest route to ulcers, sleepless nights, and nervous breakdowns, Paul not only copes with owning his numerous businesses—he is genuinely peaceful, calm, and in balance. How?

His answer is simple: He practices what he preaches. "I'm in the goal-setting business," he points out. "That's what I write about, we teach people to set and achieve personal and corporate goals. We talk about having a balanced life, and setting goals in six areas: physical, mental, spiritual, social, financial, and family. We then break those down into short-range goals, intermediate goals, and long-range goals. Then we break it down yet again into tangible goals and intangible goals. And we finally break it down into problem-solving goals and creative goals."

"I love the problem-solving goals because they give you the chance to interface with people. All growth comes from aversion or resistance, and difference. I love problems because problems give me the chance to learn something new and to grow."

"I have a private gym in my house, I swim,and I play tennis. The only way I'll stay in good shape is to put resistance against my muscles. The only way my brain will work is to put resistance against it. The only way I'm going to learn anything is to stick my neck out."

Higher Motivations

It is obvious that Paul has done extremely well in business. He claims to have more fun doing it than anyone he knows. This is very likely because his prime motivation in business is not to make himself rich. The basis of his life, he makes clear, is spiritual in nature. "My motivation for making money is the charities we support," he says.

This is not mere idle talk. Fifty percent of Paul's income goes to youth groups and Christian charitable organizations. "My wife and I are involved in several different ministries besides our church," states Paul. For example, Paul inaugurated the Passports to Success program in Waco, which guarantees college educations for all the economically-disadvantaged students in his county.

The Haggai Institute is an organization to which Paul has devoted much time and financial support. He says: "The Haggai Institute goes to Third World countries and finds Christians who are leaders, and brings them to Singapore where the skills of evangelism and leadership through a "Train the Trainer" program. Then they return to their countries as full-time evangelists, where they train an average of 100 people each. The secret of the whole program is that they aren't funded when they go back. They are taught how to raise their own money. The evangelists are not "westernized," nor are they financed by western money after the initial cost to send them to Singapore or Hawaii for training. It's the most successful program of its kind in the World today. And it's totally non-denominational. There are 105 different Christian denominations in 121 countries."

Close Family Ties

To Paul, and his wife Jane, family is what life is all about. "We have five children and 15 grandchildren," he says. We all go snow skiing once a year, and we all usually go to the Cayman Islands together once a year. We probably all get together at least once a month."

Paul is married to former Jane Gurley. Their oldest son, Jim, is a District Judge in Waco; Larry, his middle son, owns a half-dozen businesses. The youngest son, Billy, owns the renown Texas Motorples; their oldest daughter, Janna, is married to Randy Slechta, president of Leadership Management International, Inc.; and their yongerst daughter, Leslie is married to Kevin Rhea, president of L-K Marketing.

What Goes Around Comes Around

What motivates Paul to devote so much of his time, talents, and money to philanthropic activities? "First of all, these things aren't mine in the first place," he points out. "The Bible says, 'Give and it shall be given unto you.' The more you pour out, the more you have to pour. That's what it amounts to. You should spend your life helping other people, and when God gives you gifts, you should use them to help other people. My first prayer in the morning is, 'God, give me somebody that I can help today,' . . . and he usually does."

What? Me Worry?

Paul has a favorite saying about life and business that people who work around him hear often: "It's like baseball: you win some, you lose some, and some get rained out."

For the Texas entrepreneur/motivator, this is far more than a mere maxim—it's a way of living. Paul explains: "I don't take myself too seriously. I don't take business too seriously. If I've got a fault, it's that I don't worry. I imagine there are probably some things that somebody should worry about. But I have a real simple faith, and I don't worry."

At the root of Paul's "don't worry, be happy" attitude is a non-materialistic mentality. Despite his wealth, his family vacations to the Caribbean,

178

and so on, Paul takes his possessions with a grain of salt. "If we get suckered in and get fooled by our affluence, it will be the biggest mistake we've ever made," he points out. "Trust me, this stuff is all going to blow away. It's all going to rust and fall down. Absolutely the only thing we have that has any value whatsoever is our relationship with God. That's number one. And second is our love for each other as family, and our love for other people. If you put any value on anything else, you're making a mistake."

"I never, never, never give a talk to people without talking about the importance of their values. In our business we talk about success, achievement, and goals. Of course, people equate that with their careers, and their net worth, and money, and those sorts of things. I have a real strong fear that somebody will get the wrong message about the formula for success."

"My mother was the most successful person I've ever known in my life, and she was a school teacher. She spent 99.9% of her time doing things for other people. That's what I consider to be a successful person."

"The guy who takes care of the yard here at my house is one of the most successful and happiest people I know. I tell him, 'Someday I hope I can be as rich as you are.'"

Straight from the Shoulder

Advice from the man whose guidance on personal development matters is sought throughout the world is advice worth having. Imagine that you are sitting with Paul in his home. You are anxious to learn how to be truly successful, and he has a sincere interest in you. This is what he would tell you:

"First, it doesn't matter what religion you belong to or what you do. If you don't have a relationship with your Creator, you're going to have a hard time having a good relationship with other people."

"Second, you have to have the right attitude. This is what I call 'developing a servant's heart,' or 'a servant's attitude.' If you have that kind of an attitude, it doesn't matter what you are—an accountant, a musician, a banker, or an entrepreneur—you will succeed."

"Next, follow the five-point outline that I've used since I was 19 years old: First, crystallize your thinking; second, develop a plan for achieving your goal and a deadline for its attainment; third, develop a sincere desire for the things you want in life; fourth, develop supreme confidence in yourself and your own abilities; and fifth, develop a dogged determination to follow through on your plan regardless of obstacles, criticism, circumstances, or what other people say, think, or do. I call this the *Paul J. Meyer The Personal Success Plan.*"

Making a Bigger Dent

Paul loves life, "I feel like one of the luckiest people in the world," he says with unmistakable sincerity. "I have a wonderful family. I have a lot of fabulous friends and great companies. And I live in town I call 'the hub of the universe.'"

His plans for the future center around doing more of what he has been doing, because, he says, "I haven't made a dent yet. I'd like to expand everything we're doing. I'd like to do more with the Haggai Institute. I'd like to continue to help people. I'd like to do better with all the businesses we have, because I love knowing that I'm being used as an instrument to provide employment for people."

"If everybody dared to do what he most wanted to do and was most capable of doing according to his gifts, there wouldn't be any poverty and there wouldn't be any failure. My mother used to take my head and shake it and say, 'God gave you everything you need up here. It's a magic carpet and it will take you anywhere you want to go. You can be anything you want to be and have anything you want to have. All you've got to do is acknowledge that it's a gift, and develop it.'"

Now at the age when most people are coasting through retirement, Paul is gearing up for even greater roles and challenges. "I'm going to get my best idea to make a contribution to the world when I'm 85," he laughs heartily, "and I'm going to dive into it like a kid!"

Paul just recently reached the BIG 8O, and is still going strong!

Words of Wisdom and Motivation from Paul J. Meyer

- "Whatever you vividly imagine, ardently desire, sincerely believe, and enthusiastically act upon . . . must inevitably come to pass."

- "No matter who you are or what your age may be, if you want to achieve permanent sustaining success, the motivation that will drive you toward that goal must come from within. It must be personal, deep-rooted, and a part of your innermost thoughts. All other motivation—the excitement of a crowd, the stimulation of a pep talk, the exhilaration of a passing circumstance— is all external and temporary. It will not last."

- "I will never forget a particularly unsuccessful sales presentation I made. Somehow, the man I was speaking with became so angry; he walked me to the door to throw me out. I stepped outside, turned around, knocked on the door, peeked in, and said, 'Can I try again and pretend we haven't talked yet?' He didn't laugh, and I didn't make a sale, but at least I was ready with a cheerful attitude for my next interview. The ability to laugh and move on . . . was an important factor in making me successful in my business."

- "If you are not making the progress you would like to make and are capable of making, it is simply because your goals are not clearly defined."

- "Use visual reminders of your goals and the benefits they will bring to you. Pictures of your family and the members of your organization are powerful reminders of your important goals. They help you develop success attitudes. Add pictures that represent major goals you wish to attain—the home or car you want to purchase, the office building you want to build, places you want to go, or personality traits you wish to develop."

- "The world is God's storehouse of abundance. You can go to it with a pickup truck, a bucket, a shovel, a cup, or a spoon. Or you can, like a lot of people I know, go with a sieve. They expect nothing and they get nothing."

ADDENDUM D

Beyond Super Leverage: The Quickest Path to a Billion Dollars

by Mark O. Haroldsen

Not many people set goals to become a billionaire. That's an awfully big number—one I only briefly thought about for myself. For me there are other things I wanted to do with my life. BUT . . .

I know that I could have done it if I had wanted to and I know how to do it and what it takes to get there.

For the very, very few who want to get to that rare and lofty place, I will tell you what it takes to get there, but let me make two points first.

ONE—The strategy and steps I'm about to disclose can certainly be used by anyone regardless of how large of fortune he or she wants to create—whether it's a few million or one hundred million, it works just as well.

TWO—Just a comment to let you know how truly rare it is to reach that billion dollar mark. As I write this, there are under 300 billionaires in the United States, and only 497 billionaires in the world. That's only one out of every 12,877,263 people on the planet who have ever reached that status.

So how does a person starting with nothing reach the rarified air of a billionaire or even one tenth of that amount?

Here's how: It's what I call "beyond super leverage" and it must be done by leveraging both money and people.

It's all well and good for you to buy an income producing piece of real estate with 10 or 20 percent of your own money and 80 percent of borrowed money, which will make you a ton of dough if you buy right and manage the property well. However, to move to a much higher level and in short order, you need to do more.

Most people, once they've figured out how leverage can lift their net worth so quickly, they go to the next step. It can also be very risky. They often borrow the 80 or 90 percent the bank lends them, and in some cases they also borrow the 10 or 20 percent down payment. This, of course, puts them in a 100 percent financed position. That's all well and good as long as everything goes almost perfect with the property. A slight hiccup with the economy or an unforeseen problem with that particular property could cause you to lose it all.

If you want to go for the tens of millions level, or a hundred million, or even a billion, you may need a better plan?

The Billion-Dollar Hansen Model

The Dell Loy Hansen model is an ideal model for such a goal. Instead of borrowing the down payment and using that kind of super leverage (and risk), you simply have partners put up all or part of the down payment. If you take time to cultivate good, wealthy partners and treat them well, you will have a never-ending and actually increasing source of equity capital.

In many cases, Dell Loy Hansen and his partners used a much larger down payment than 20 percent. Why? First of all, people with a lot of money usually don't want a high-risk investment. The quickest way to scare off big money people is to try to sell them a deal that "promises them" a ridiculously high return for their passive investment—for example: "You're going to double your money in the first year."

By using larger down payments with partners' money, you can decrease the overall risk for everyone. Yes, the overall return for the partners is less, but if the deal is structured right—and fair—I should add, the return can be much greater. Of course, the reason for your high return is because you have less of your own money in the deal and maybe not even any cash in the deal at all. It's not that you haven't put anything into the deal. You've put time, energy, and effort, along with your skill and know-how to find the deal and put it together.

People with a lot of cash usually are satisfied with lower returns that are paid regularly and consistently. They know that very high rates of return

184

without hands-on efforts are virtually non-existent. To offer them high numbers (like 100 percent per year), even if you think you can deliver them, is a huge mistake.

Remember, high returns are certainly possible for those of us who work our tails off, but for the passive investors (those who just put up the money and wait for their monthly check) normally cannot nor do they expect to get high returns.

You see, Hansen has learned that lesson. If a big money investor goes into one of his deals with a projected cash return of . . . let's say, 9 percent . . . and that investor knows that the total down payment of all the equity partners totals 40 percent, that investor feels pretty darn safe. Dell Loy Hansen is a near genius when it comes to his grasp of the numbers and putting together pro formas as to a property's potential.

Then when Hansen delivers a cash return of 12 or 14 percent, or even 19 percent, WOW! That investor is calling all his friends, and making sure he puts his kids' trust money into the next deal . . . and Hansen doesn't have to look too far for investors on his next deal. In many cases, Hansen puts some of his own money into his deals, but if he wanted to, he could legitimately give himself a fair piece of each deal without putting up any cash.

Either way, that's what I call it "beyond super leverage." And that's exactly the first step toward the multi-, multi-millions or even a billion.

However, I should note that by Hansen putting up at least some of his own money, it does send a very good message to all the investors and makes it much easier to get partners into his deals, especially if it's the first deal a new partner has with Hansen.

So with that basic overview of the general plan of what can be done, let me give you the exact steps of how to go about it—and then a list of the human traits, skills, and qualities that a person needs to have to get the job done. And remember, you can use the following steps to end up with $1 million, $10 million, or $100 million—those numbers being far short of the billion dollar mark, but still pretty darn satisfying in anyone's book.

Stay Away from Investment Time Suckers

Before we go to the required steps, let me make a comment about the best types of investments that will most likely serve your purposes of reaching the extreme levels of net worth. Most people don't realize one of the critical ingredients to super success, especially in the investment arena, is this thing we call "time." It's a must, if you really want to hit it big, to stay with investments that don't suck your time. If you stay with investments that are not "time suckers," then it frees up your time so you have more time to add to your investments. I know so many people who go out and invest in small businesses which almost inevitably take enormous amounts of time, thus they are "time-tied" to those small business and don't have time to add to their portfolio and hence never rise to the next level.

But now, let's look at the human traits, skills, desired qualities, and the required steps:

The Desired Qualities

As you read this list and compare yourself with this ideal person, or what we'll call the "Billion-Dollar Man or Women," keep in mind that no one rates a perfect 10 on each of these attributes, skills, or qualities. But on the other hand, if you rate yourself a 1 or 2 on each of these qualities, you'd better not quit your day job, just yet.

1. High energy level.
2. High honesty and integrity level.
3. Ability to explain and excite people about potential (salesmanship).
4. Very good to "super" organized.
5. A firm grasp of the numbers as it relates to the property's return and potential return.
6. Jack-of-all-trades and master of none.
7. A good reader of people and not only an ability to negotiate without showing all the cards, but also have the ability to hire and keep talented people as employees or associates.
8. Must be good at delegation and following up on those to whom you delegate to make sure the job gets done.

The Seven Required Steps

1. Find it.
2. Negotiate it.
3. Tie it up.
4. Package it.
5. Share it/Sell it.
6. Manage it (very well).
7. Duplicate it.

A few thoughts about the Seven Required Steps:

1. Find it. There are numerous was to locate income properties. From using the "shotgun" approach to using top-notch brokers and agents, there are plenty of properties available to choose from. Now don't forget, one of the quickest ways to find properties of virtually any type, from apartments to office buildings, is to go on the Internet. Just go to Google® or any other good search engine site, and type in "real estate listings" or "apartments for sale" or "homes for sale" or any words that might lead you to the kind of properties you're looking for. Most sites you will be directed to will allow you to go to any city in the United States and then enter in the price range you desire.

Concerning brokers or agents, I think you will be amazed, as I have been, once you find and connect with those rare high volume, high quality producing brokers and agents, how many great properties they seem to uncover and bring to you.

2. Negotiate it. Once you've found a property that fits your approximate criteria, and one, of course, that you know can deliver the numbers to keep your partners very satisfied, you must push as hard and as smart as you possibly can to get the best price and terms. There are a lot of different negotiating strategies to use and generally you need to use the one that fits your personality best. Some people, like Dell Loy Hansen (who, by the way, is an excellent and tough negotiator), like to negotiate face-to-face and are good at it. Personally, I don't do as well with the face-to-face negotiations. My face gives too much away—in other words, I am not a good bluffer in person. However, I do very well on the phone or even better on

paper with the broker or agent acting as a go between and doing the face-to-face for me.

You need to know yourself well and use a negotiating style that fits you. But remember this—negotiating the deal is a huge part of the battle, and if you do it well, you'll be able to deliver the rate of return that will keep partners knocking at your door and wanting in on your next deal. And I don't care what a seller or buyer says about "this is my final price." Virtually, every price is negotiable. Having said that, however, if you know the asking price is truly a deal and will give you the return you need, don't be greedy, because you just might lose out to another buyer

3. Tie it up. Here are a few ways to "tie up a property:" Tie it up with "subject to" language. The standards, of course, are these:

<u>This offer is subject to:</u>

a. Inspection within so many days—the longer the better.

b. Review of the income and expenses and acceptance of same.

c. Financing that is acceptable to buyer.

d. My partner's approval within three or four weeks or more if you think the seller will agree. (This is my favorite "subject to.")

By using any of the above or maybe all of the above and putting as long a time frame on it as possible, this gives you time to package it and share it (sell it).

4. Package it. Now that you have the property "tied up," you want to put what you've tied up into a package that makes it simple for the investor to see what he's going to "buy in to."

This package would include the numbers and the pictures—numbers such as the income and expenses as they are now—plus a proforma (projection) of several years into the future. That is what can reasonably be done to increase income and decrease expenses, and therefore increase the rate of return to your investors.

These numbers, put together with a well-thought-out summary and description of the property—along with photos that show off the property, of course—are a critical part of the package.

188

5. Share it/Sell it. The packaging done in Step Four is critical. But even more critical is your energy, integrity, and ability to excite people and convince them you can and will deliver what you so promise.

Just about anyone can figure out where the big money people are, but if you don't have the qualities listed above, you won't get past the receptionist.

Networking is key here. If you have friends who are CPAs, tax attorneys, real estate agents or brokers, and CEOs or VPs in different companies, you've got the basis of a great start. Each one of them has friends and clients they can refer you to, but only if these people trust your judgment, your integrity, and your ability to deliver what you say. If you do your first deal right (and your first deal will no doubt be your toughest), the world will beat a pathway to your door.

6. Manage it. This step is the hardest one, and one that, for many—including myself—is not a lot of fun.

That step is the hard knock, day-to-day, every single day, school of good consistent property management. With more and more property coming in on the plan I've outlined above, you must learn to tap very good people to help with the management of all those properties. You must delegate, delegate, delegate, and to keep those good people you must have very attractive incentives for each one of them in order for them to produce and keep them happy.

Dell Loy Hansen has hundreds of young, ambitious, and well-trained people managing all of his properties. Sure, some of them leave and some are sent packing—and it's a constant battle. But it's a battle that needs to be fought, if you want both the rewards and in the rewards of great satisfaction and contribution.

7. Duplicate it. Great fortunes are made again and again by doing "what works" again and again. Once you've built your mold (and realize it's never a perfect mold and you're always tweaking it) keep using that mold over and over. If you can buy one great deal, package it, share it, and manage it, you certainly can do it a second and third and fourth time.

So many people buy one great property—think they were just lucky and stop there. Then years later, they look back and say, "Wow, look what I've done with this house, or duplex, or small office building. Gee, I wish I had bought 10 of them back then."

Don't be that person. Keep on keeping on—duplicate your successes.

ADDENDUM E

High Rates of Return That Make You Rich

by Mark O. Haroldsen

A famous and wealthy man, Andrew Carnegie once said, "Ninety percent of all millionaires become so through owning real estate. More money has been made in real estate than in all industrial investments combined. The wise young man or wage earner of today invests his money in real estate."

There is a multitude of different types and sizes of real estate investments. And there are even more people representing these investments, vying for our investment dollar. But of the hundreds of available investments I know of, none offer as many basic advantages as real estate. These advantages put the odds overwhelmingly in your favor for succeeding in the pursuit of wealth. The four basic advantages of real estate, which we talk about in detail later, are:

(1) Cash flow that is usually higher than in other investments;

(2) Equity buildup that can dramatically increase the overall return;

(3) Inflation, both natural and forced;

(4) A tax shelter that very few other investments offer.

The odds are heavily in your favor. William Nickerson, author of the best selling book *How I Turned $1000 into Five Million in Real Estate—in My Spare Time*, thinks real estate is the best investment because it is so easy to use other people's money. As he puts it:

> Most forms of investment pay only the paltry leavings after others deduct their expenses and fair compensation for using your money. You lend your

savings to banks, and insurance companies, and they capitalize on your money for their profit.

Investment in business and income property puts you on the real money-making side of the capital fence and pays you for courage and imagination. You profit not only from your own savings but also from the savings of the timid, the uninformed, and the satiated who already possess all the money they want.

Every venture presents an element of risk, but with rent-producing income property, you take negligible risks and your chances for success are 1,600 times better, for example, than your chances if you start in business. With each, however, you follow the freeway that leads to wealth by harnessing the secret force of capitalism—which is the pyramiding power of borrowed money. Regardless of how wisely you invest, you can't go far on your own money. Your greatest expansion is assured by making maximum use of the other fellow's money.

The road to riches is paved with borrowed money. Big-time real estate operators buy properties worth millions without putting in a penny of their own. Multi-million-dollar deals are made by borrowing the utmost from mortgages and the balance on personal and collateral notes. (*How I Turned $1,000 into Five Million in Real Estate—in My Spare Time,* p. 13.)

Nickerson got his figures—the odds of 1,600 to 1—from the Department of Commerce, which states that 4 out of 5 new businesses fail within eight years. Additionally, 50 percent go out of business within two years. The overall odds are 4 to 1 that a new business will not make it. He contrasts those with real estate investments, where only 1 out of 400 properties is foreclosed, establishing the odds of 400 to 1 in favor of you succeeding. By combining these two sets of statistics, he came up with 1,600 to 1 odds for success in income property.

In addition to the four basic advantages of real estate, two others reduce the risk of loss. First, housing is a basic necessity. Most investments, such as stocks, bonds, motels, hotels, resorts, and miscellaneous businesses, do not have this advantage. Those investments normally are made when basic necessities have already been taken care of. Virtually every person in this country wants to upgrade his housing by moving into something nicer, thus creating a constant demand and a demand that only moves upward.

This demand is increased by the birth rate and by new families formed through marriage. In some areas there is the added benefit of the movement of people from one state to another. The Western states and the Sun Belt in the last 15 to 20 years have benefited most by such migration. Current statistics show this pattern continuing with these states having the greatest percentage increases.

With this advantage, it is difficult to fail with ownership of income properties. Even without the advantage of migration of people into your state or community the odds of success are heavily in your favor.

The second big advantage is the control one has with income properties.

With stocks, you not only do not control the market and the fluctuation of the market, you do not even control the corporation in which you have invested. If the president of the corporation makes an unwise decision, you have no recourse (assuming you do not have controlling interest). In the ownership of income-producing properties, you do not have absolute control over the market; however, through the management of your property over which you have 100 percent control, and have complete freedom to better your position if necessary.

Your primary concern in projecting the growth of your net worth should be the return on equity (the return you get from investing whatever dollars you have). Specifically, all you care about is the overall return you receive when you add up the four advantages of real estate: (1) cash flow, (2) equity buildup, (3) inflation, and (4) tax shelter or tax advantages.

Cash Flow—To Reinvest, Not Spend

First of all, cash flow in real estate investing can be very high and has consistently been higher than other types of investments. Cash flow can make a tremendous difference in the rate of growth in acquiring a fortune.

It is simple to calculate the cash flow figure. You need only two answers: (1) How much out-of-pocket money did you put into the investment? (2) How much money did you get out of the deal (put in your pocket) in one year? If you put in $5,000 cash and took out $1,000 in one year, your cash flow was 20 percent ($1,000 ÷ $5,000 = 20 percent). Cash flow is the first thing you should look for in evaluating a real estate investment. Remember, if you get an extremely high cash flow, you can take that cash and reinvest it in another similar investment. This gives the compounding effect to your money and can work miracles in a short period of time.

Equity Buildup—Adds to Your Wealth Monthly

The second advantage to real estate investments is the equity buildup or the amount of principal payment made to reduce a mortgage loan. This payment, of course, is made from the gross income (rental income from tenants of your properties), unless you paid cash for the property. Of course, then all the cash flow goes into your pocket to reinvest.

But equity buildup by mortgage pay down provides a great return for you, even if you buy that property with a lot of leverage—let's say a 10 to 1 ratio, and again, if the numbers are too small for your thinking, just add a zero to each figure. Let's assume for our illustration, you bought a $100,000 property with $10,000 down and the remaining $90,000 borrowed at 6.5 percent for 20 years. Now watch the return on your down payment jump.

The first year equity buildup through mortgage pay down would be $2,268.00. This added equity will give you a return on your cash down of 22.68 percent that first year. But later on this equity jumps as the principal allocation of each payment increases. You would receive a whopping 40.66 percent return in equity buildup in the 10th year alone. And that's before we take into account the next two factors: inflation and tax advantage.

Forced Inflation and Natural Appreciation Will Make You Richer

Inflation or appreciation is the third ingredient that adds to the overall return of investments in real estate, even when inflation is seemingly a very low 2 or 3 percent. There are several causes of inflation. Without trying to debate who and what causes inflation, there is no question that continued deficit spending by our government is a prime factor. But whatever the causes, there can be benefits to inflation if the investor realizes proper and wise use of leverage. Let me illustrate with a very simplified example. Say, again, you bought a $100,000 piece of income-producing property. Assume you paid $10,000 down, with the $90,000 balance owing to either the seller or through a mortgage to a bank, and possibly a second mortgage. You would begin making monthly payments on the mortgages. These would be made from the rents you collect each month.

Even if you didn't have any cash left over at the end of each month (cash flow), after making the payments, what would be your situation, assuming that this particular piece of real estate inflated for whatever reason by 10 percent in one year?

First of all, what would the building be worth at the end of the first year? With simple mathematics, it is obvious the building would be worth $110,000. By subtracting the $90,000 mortgage or less because of payments toward the principal (equity buildup), the balance would equal your new net equity in the building. What has this 10 percent inflation done to your return (assuming you were to sell the building)? The magic of leverage can be seen in this simple example. Even though the building only grew in worth by 10 percent, your return was an astounding 100 percent, on inflation alone.

It is not likely that real estate by itself will appreciate or inflate at a 10 percent rate per year. Depending on the area in the country and loca-tions within particular towns, the rate of so-called natural inflation has been anywhere from 1.5 percent to 4.5 percent per year.

There is another kind of inflation, however, that really should not be called inflation, but that's what I call it. What I call forced inflation could probably more properly be called appreciation through improvements. Forced inflation can be used over and over again in virtually every city and also in concert with natural inflation. What forced inflation does is simple: It creates higher worth of a particular real estate investment (income prop-erty), brought about by improvements to that property. Using the former example of a $100,000 building that improved in value by 10 percent in one year—if this building were to actually inflate in value only 2 percent in a given year and your improvement goal called for an increase in net equities of 100 percent, you would have to do something to bring about an increase in value of $10,000.00. And you could likely do that through cosmetic improvements, such as paint, carpet, etc. Of course, those improvements take cash or a loan on the property. The additional cost of these improvements need to be added to your down payment in calculating your rate of return. But these improvements may lift the value way beyond their costs.

Even if one plans on only the natural inflation, and assuming that infla-tion is a 2 percent factor on the $100,000 property, this is still a 20 percent rate of return on the original $10,000 investment (2 percent on $100,000 equals $2,000 annually; this $2,000 would be a 20 percent return on the original $10,000 down payment). The extra rate of return, derived from inflation when added to cash flow and equity buildup, makes our real estate investment an unusual and attractive way to invest money. Of course, if we stop after one or two investments in real estate, we don't get the compounding effect.

Tax Shelter: Short Cut to Wealth

The fourth fact that makes real estate investments so attractive and adds immensely to the overall return is tax shelter or tax advantages. Let me ask a simple question: How long would it take a person to make $1million starting with $10,000 and investing the money at a consistent 25 percent compounded rate of return? I will even help you out by providing a chart at the end of this addendum. By using the chart, the obvious answer would be 21 years. Right? Wrong! Why? Because of that government agency we are all familiar with—the IRS. Yes, Uncle Sam takes a big part, an ever-growing part, of our income.

To answer the above question, we must know two additional facts: What income tax bracket is the person in and what type of investments is he making? Let's make two assumptions: This person is in a 50 percent tax bracket (this also assumes these investments are not held long enough to be long-term capital gains and the 50 percent rate is the state tax rate added on top of the maximum federal tax rate) and is making general types of investments in stocks and bonds and various small businesses. Okay, and now the question again: How long would it take this person to make $1 million with $10,000 compounding at 25 percent? If you want to take the time to figure it, the simple way is just to compound $10,000 at an annual rate of 12.5 percent.

The answer could be stated this way: If the person were 30 years of age when he began this program, made the investments we mentioned and paid average taxes, he would be 70 years old by the time he reached the $1 million-dollar mark. It would have taken him 40 years.

Now, compare the man who made real estate investments, paid no tax because of the preferential treatment he can take advantage of, and he reaches the goal by age 51, or in 21 years. Through the wise use of current tax laws, one person was able to enjoy his fortune 19 years longer than the one who did not take advantage of the same tax laws.

One of the greatest tax inventions given to us was the IRS designation of the 1031 Exchange Rule which allows a real estate investor to pay zero tax on the sale of a property as long as that investor follows the 1031 Rules very strictly and invests the proceeds from the sale into another "like kind property" within the prescribed time limits. That is, you must put the proceeds from the sale of a property into what is commonly called an exchange company (the actual name the IRS uses for this type of company is Qualified Accommodator). The proceeds are deposited into the exchange company directly from the closing of the sale of your property. The proceeds can never be in your control. You must then identify up to three other properties that you may buy using the proceeds from the sale of the first property. You have 45 days to identify the three properties and notify the exchange company in writing of those properties. Then you have another 135 days to close on one or more of the three properties you identified using the proceeds being held by the exchange company. The bottom line is that you don't have to pay any capital gains tax—you simply defer it. You can defer subsequent capital gains should you sell the new property by following the same 1031 Exchange rules into another new property. In fact, you can do this over and over through the end of your life, and even beyond that if you do some smart tax and estate planning. So, in theory, you will never have to pay tax on those properties if you do it right.

Believe It

When the four basic types of return in a real estate investment are tabulated, the total potential seems almost unbelievable and unachievable. Whereas it is difficult to find real estate investments that have the high side of the range in all four categories (225 percent), it is not impossible and can be done regularly if enough effort is put into the task. Below is a tabulation of the four ingredients to real estate investment:

Type of Return	Annual Percentage Rate of Return on Beginning Equity
Cash Flow	5% to 25%
Equity Buildup	3% to 45%
Inflation (mostly forced)	10% to 105%
Tax Advantage	2% to 50%
	20% to 225%

To many people, the range of 20 percent on the low side, to 225 percent on the high side seems too optimistic for the total return on equity. Believe me, these are not pie-in-the-sky figures. These are down-to-earth figures and are achievable on a consistent basis. Where you end up on that scale is up to you and depends on how much effort you put into locating the right investment, bargaining for the price and terms, buying the property, making necessary changes, and disposing of the property in a way that is advantageous from a tax standpoint.

Some might question whether it is worth the effort to try to reach the higher end of the scale—225 percent. If that is your attitude, I suggest you sit down with a calculator and find the results on any size investment with a 225 percent compound rate of return. I think you will find enough motivation from your calculations to answer whether it is worth the effort to you.

In my program, I have not yet reached the high end of the scale. In my early years, with smaller amounts of money, I achieved an overall return of a little better than 160 percent. On individual investments I have reached the 225 percent mark. I know others who have hit the high mark consistently so I know it can be done. If you are the ambitious and persistent type, you might well be one who can do it. Even if you only muster out at a 20 percent or 30 percent return and stick with it, your million-dollar daydream will become a reality. Now after nearly 40 years of investing, my overall average return has been more than 30% compounded annually, which has earned me many, many millions of dollars.

And those returns can be pumped even higher for you if you bring in partners. (For more information on the wise use of partners, read Addendum D.)

Accidental Fortune

When it comes to investments, some research shows that most people make more money by accident in real estate, than they do on purpose in almost any other type of investment.

Over the years I have observed that this is especially true when it comes to real estate vs. stocks. And there is a simple reason for real estate working out very well for most people vs. stock investments.

The answer lies in the nature of all of us humans—we all think pretty much alike when it comes to risk and reward—and fear and greed.

Human Nature and the Stock Market

For example, let's say a person buys $10,000 worth of stock and it goes up in value to $20,000 or $30,000-what would most people do? What would you do? Most people would sell it thinking that they don't want to see it fall back to where they bought it. Yes, some people might hold it until it was worth maybe $40,000 or $50,000 before selling—but in any case, the higher it rises the more pressure the typical human mind feels to sell.

The point is, most humans reason in their minds that they've got to sell it and lock in their profit. But many times those stocks are the very ones that turn out to be the Microsoft companies of the world—and 10 or 15 years later, that $10,000 investment is worth a half million or even $1 million dollars. But of course, they didn't profit from the rise because they sold their stock.

I think it would be pretty safe to say that there are very, very few people who bought Microsoft on the initial public offering, who held it through the years to its very pinnacle or even close.

And guess what? When most people buy stock and it goes down in value, once again they usually do the exact opposite of what they should do. They hold on to it! Not only because of ego and not wanting to admit they were wrong, but because they hope that if they hold on to it long enough, it will go back up to where they can at least break even. (I guess people think "what goes down, must go up"—Hmmm, go figure that one.)

In both cases it's a big mistake—a huge mistake!

By selling stock, that goes up, too early, and holding on to the ones that go down, eventually and inevitably, you will end up with a portfolio full of "losers."

But why don't people make the same mistake with real estate?

Real Estate Fits Your Mindset

Overall, it's because of the nature of real estate—especially developed real estate with income flowing from it. Everyone can relate to real estate as a necessity. It also fits in or blends in with the emotional and mental makeup of a typical human being.

What do I mean by that? Just this:

First, we like, and can identify with, what we can drive by, see, touch, admire, maybe live in, fix up, take pictures of, collect rent from, and show to our family and friends.

Second, we don't easily know on a day-to-day, or week-to-week, or even a month-to-month basis exactly what that real estate is worth, so we don't have a thought or an urge to sell it.

Third, even if we think it's worth more, it takes a lot of effort to sell it. We must advertise it and/or list it. Get it ready to be shown. Show it—usually many times. And go through lots of other hassles.

Bottom line, since we don't easily know the short-term market fluctuations, and because it's cumbersome and time-consuming to sell real estate, we tend to hold on to it for a very long time—and that usually turns out to be a good thing.

Consequently, more people make more money in real estate by accident than they do on purpose in most other investments.

From Olympic Gold Medal to Golden Rewards

Now here's an incredible true-life story of a super real estate success caused by the factors I've just mentioned above:

Recently I was talking to my very dear friends Stein and Francoise Eriksen about my new book on real estate that was 99 percent finished and just a few weeks from going to press.

Now, Stein and Francoise are both super successful, fun, and dynamic people. Their success stems from Stein's Olympic Gold Medal and World Cup Skiing Title years ago (he was the first superstar of skiing). They also attribute much success from Francoise' fiery Frenchwoman's drive and personality that have garnered much attention in the retail world of ski apparel.

These two people, along with a great third partner—their very bright and energetic son, Bjorn—make a terrific trio!

But what I didn't know until my recent conversation was that a HUGE contribution to their overall financial success came from a little real estate investment made many years ago—and made almost by accident.

First, I'll give you the monthly bottom line—(which I think will make you want to read on). Their bottom line is $50,000 that comes in automatically each and every month. That's a pretty nice bottom line—and that's pretty nice passive income that started somewhat by accident.

It started in Aspen, Colorado, where Stein had a ski shop and was paying $2,000 a month in rent. Out of the blue, a friend who owned one-half interest in a building on the main street of Aspen called Stein and asked him if he wanted to buy his one-half interest. It seems that Stein's friend wanted to do some major traveling through Europe and other parts of the world.

Stein told him that he would love to buy the building but he couldn't afford it. Not to be deterred, his friend said, "Wait a minute . . . how much in rent are you paying each month now? What if you could move your shop into my building and pay me the same on the purchase of my building rather than throwing money away on rent?"

That sounded pretty good to Stein, but what about the down payment? Where would that come from?

A $25,000 down payment was worked out, and Stein had to scramble hard to put that much money together but finally managed to do it.

And now, many years later, through the ups, downs, and sideways markets, Stein still owns the property and gladly collects his hassle-free $50,000 net income *per month* from his free and clear building. (He did buy the other half interest in the building three years later for the same price that he paid for the first half.)

Fast forward to the year 2008. That year, Stein's Aspen property was exchanged by using the 1031 Section of the Tax Code for quite a few smaller properties in several Western States, which nearly doubled the amount of monthly net income to the family

Now here's the $100,000 question. If that had been $25,000 worth of Microsoft stock (plus a $2,000 monthly payment), do you think Stein, or you, or I might have been tempted to sell our position along the way—maybe when it doubled or tripled, or quintupled in valued—especially if we could have made that sale by simply picking up the phone and calling a broker, or hitting a few keys on our computer to make the sale?

I'm not sure about Stein's answer or yours—but I think I would have sold way too soon! And to think some people have called me a "Financial Genius."

No, I'm just an ordinary guy. But I chose an extraordinary vehicle called improved real estate that makes me look like a "Financial Genius" as it makes my bank account bulge.

Example of Compounding

($10,000 at 25 percent for 21 years)

Years	
0	$ 10,000
1	12,500
2	15,600
3	19,531
4	24,414
5	30,500
6	38,125
7	47,656
8	59,500
9	74,375
10	92,969
11	116,125
12	145,156
13	181,445
14	226,250
15	282,812
16	353,515
17	441,259
18	551,562
19	689,453
20	861,250
21	$1,076,562

NOTE: Several of the above figures have been rounded off for ease in figuring.

ADDENDUM F

Random Thoughts

By Mark Haroldsen

I recently went through my journals, which I've kept for 46 years, and I've picked out what I think, for me, are some real gems. So I'm going to share them with you now.Since I really do believe we are all just one—living totally interdependently on this planet—I felt it appropriate and potentially helpful, as I complete this book, to share some additional random thoughts that have motivated me.

- If we don't like where we are in our lives, we have to first change the nature of our thinking to change the outcome.

- If our inner-peace is the most important thing to us, then we must work on ways to ensure that no one can shake that inner-peace.

- We love purely when we release people to be who they are.

- Mother Teresa said, "There are not great deeds, just small deeds done with great love."

- The most enlightened prayer is not, "Dear God, send me someone wonderful." It is, "Dear God, help me realize that I am someone wonderful."

- When we have the choice to be right or be kind, always go with being kind.

- To forgive and let go is the only way out of hell.

- To attempt to create what we want without passion is like dressing up a corpse.

- The currency to attack what we want in our lives is our thoughts.

- We cannot manifest what we want by focusing on what we don't want or what we hate.

- Always have two books: one to read from and one to write into.

- Our great ideas and thoughts are bound to be remembered.

- The greatest book ever written is your own book—about you.

- To be vulnerable means plunging into the fear—the wonderful pay-off is that we become our own great source of strength.

- In our vulnerability lies our power. It's where dreams begin.

- The very nature of creating something is that we never know what we are doing.

- Goodness and love assure us that our lives really mattered.

- It seems that all our dreams that are set into the form of specific goals have magic to them and give us numerous benefits that go on and on.

We experience love in the form of:

- Kindness

- Giving

- Mercy

- Compassion

- Peace

- Joy

- Acceptance

- Non-judgment

- Intimacy

We act out or experience fear in the form of:

- Anger
- Abuse
- Disease
- Pain
- Greed
- Addiction
- Selfishness
- Obsession
- Corruption
- Violence
- War
- Ridicule
- Manipulation
- Abuse of power